Basic Concepts of The Qur'an

Mawlana Abul Kalam Azad

Preparead By

Dr. Syed Abdul Latif : President of Academy of Islamic studies and the Institute of Indo Middle East Cultural Studies, Hyderabad, India

Qadeem Press

Qadeem Press

Qadeem Press Edition
Breathing Life into Forgotten Pages
www.qadeempress.com

Reprinted by Qadeem Press in 2025

Find our titles on your favourite online bookstore using the keyword 'Qadeem Press'

To the Memory
Of him
Whose views are embodied in this Volume,
Of him
Who had read the matter it contained,
prior to its going to the press,
But who, ere it came out of it,
Went to his rest,

To waken, as the Qur'ān envisages,
Into a life of deeper realizations
—' *From state to state, shall ye,*
assuredly, be carried forward.'—

(*Qur'ān* 84 : 19)

Dedicated
In his moment of sorrow
By one
Who sadly misses his presence here.

22nd June 1958. SYED ABDUL LATIF.

PREFACE

Since about the middle of the 19th century, numerous attempts have been made by Muslim scholars to interpret the Qur'ān to the modern world. By far the largest output of literature produced in this connection, whether in the form of commentaries, critiques, or articles in periodicals, has been in Urdu, English and Arabic. But whatever the medium of expression employed, the net result is still far from satisfactory. The modernists have mostly tried to square the Quranic meaning with the thought-content of the culture of Europe, even as some of the commentators of the early centuries of Islam had tried under the influence of the Greek literature translated into Arabic to square it with the philosophic speculations of Greece. Only spasmodically or in flashes have stray corners of the Quranic message been exposed to view in its reality. At any rate, no sustained effort has been made by them to let the Qur'ān speak for itself. Warmed up by the efforts of the modernists, the orthodox 'Ulama too have no doubt tried to appear modern in their latest approaches to the Qur'ān. But the dead weight of the medieval obscurantism which has for ages clung to the Muslim religious thought has proved too heavy for them to throw off. It was only as late as 1930, a ray of hope was furnished by the appearance of the first volume of the Tarjumān-al-Qur'ān of Mawlana Abul Kalam Azad, of which the Commentary of Sūrat-ul-Fātiḥa formed the opening section, wherein a serious attempt was made to restore to the Quranic word the meaning that it was originally meant to bear.

The most characteristic feature of the Qur'ān, it may be stated, is its method of presentation. It is simple and direct. It does not employ any artifice, nor display any conventional poses. Its appeal is to the elemental feeling and imagination of man, and to his daily experiences of life. It presents, so to say, a heart to heart talk between God and man couched in a language simple enough to be understood by the common man. Such is the method adopted by the Qur'ān, a method common to all revealed scriptures. But this method, important as it was, was rarely the subject of regular study in any Muslim seminar or seat of learning in the past. 'Fadhakkir-bil-Qur'ān '—' explain the Qur'ān in the manner of the Qur'ān' (Q. 50:45)—was the directive furnished by the Qur'ān itself. But the directive except in the early days of Islam never was seriously observed in the course of history. The tragedy of the Qur'ān is that no sooner had the first generation of believers passed away, even before the second century of the Hijra was over, the influence of Greek thought introduced through translations of Greek works on philosophy and science began to close round the Muslim mind. The simplicity of the original approach to the Qur'ān in consequence gave way to dialectical disquisition, so much so, that the commentaries of the Qur'ān which now came to be written by Muslim scholars invested the Quranic word, as Mawlana Azad explains at length in his preface to the first edition of the Tarjumān-al-Qur'ān with a meaning which it was not meant to bear.

The Qur'ān, be it remembered, was not a planned production. It was delivered piece-meal during the course of 23 years as warranted by the changing circumstances of the Prophet's mission. Those who first responded to its call and successfully implemented its directions were the persons whose interpretation of the Quranic word should naturally have been regarded as standard interpretation. But the commentators of the Qur'ān who came after them, side-tracked their inter-pretation, and began to read new meanings into it. The tendency came to be ever on the increase, as new races came to embrace Islam bringing with them the memories of their former faiths. The result was the rise of a bewildering variety of views concerning the teaching of the Qur'ān. The plain meaning of the plain word gradually went out of fashion, and the allegorical or figurative element in the Qur'ān came to bear either a literal sense or a sense alien to the very spirit of the Quranic ideology. 'The impact' as the writer has observed elsewhere, 'was partly pagan in character reflected in the anthropomorphic touches imparted to the concept of Divinity and its attributes, and partly mystic in significance as inspired essentially by Neo-Platonism and manifested chiefly in the Ajami or non-Arab attempt to read esoteric meaning into what was basically exoteric or mundane in the Qur'ān.'* To make matters worse, with the close of the 4th century of the Hijra, the intellectual movement stimu-lated so far by foreign influences, received a set-back. The pendulam swung to the other end. A reaction set in, and limits were fixed for everything in every sphere of life and thought. This is not the place to go into the history of this development or of the forces which brought it about. Suffice it to say that from this time onward, a period began wherein it was not permissible to strike out any fresh line of approach to the Qur'ān. The commentaries of the Qur'ān produced under the new

* "The Mind Al-Qur'ān Builds." The Academy of Islamic studies, Agapura, Hyderabad, India, 1952, p. 5.

order were more or less mere reproductions of earlier attempts or imitative in character. The imitation, as Mawlana Azad observes in his preface referred to above, was very often in favour of the abstruse, fantastic and out of the ordinary. Few cared to point to the simplicity of the Qur'ān and its directness. Religion, if it was to bear that name, was expected to be something mysterious. That was the conception which came into vogue, a conception which, among the orthodox, persists even till this day. The commentaries of Razi and Baiḍawi who set the model still hold the field. It is this heritage of inept evaluation, the legacy of the past, that Mawlana Azad has tried to counter in his writings, particularly in his commentary of the Sūrat-ul-Fātiḥa which is intended to serve as an introduction to the study of the Qur'ān.

Although the best part of Mawlana Azad's life was spent actively in the forefront of India's struggle for freedom, marked by periods of incarceration in jails, it is remarkable that he should have managed, in the midst of his ordeals, to nurse zealously his inherent talent for scholarship and produce a body of literature which has won for him an established place in the field of Islamic learning. His searching enquiries into the Quranic teachings have disclosed to him the realistic humanism that it stands for. It is this humanism imbibed from the Quran which he applies back to the study of every detail of its message. In fact, when one goes out of his Quranic studies and looks into the discourses delivered by him at various learned gatherings, one is struck by the touch that he invariably gives of this humanism to the solution of the numerous political and cultural problems which face the world of today.

Mawlana Azad's Quranic studies have taken various

forms, the most important of them being his monumental work entitled 'Tarjumān-al-Qur'ān' running into three volumes, two of which have already been published. The work is an explanatory translation of the Qur'ān in Urdu supported by foot-notes in the form of commentary, the underlying purpose of which is to re-create for the world of today the meaning which the Quranic word was taken to mean when it was delivered. To facilitate an easy grasp of the Quranic attitudes, he has under the very first chapter, the Sūrat-ul-Fātiḥa, discussed the basic concepts that it presents which in one form or other recur throughout the Qur'ān, and which together constitute its ideology.

What is noteworthy in his discourse is the distinction which he makes between this ideology and the manner or method of implementing it or the programme pursued thereunder. The one he calls Dīn, and the other Shar'a and Minhāj, terms which the Qur'ān itself furnishes. The former, viz., the Dīn, as the Qur'ān asserts, was given to every community or section of mankind through chosen men called Prophets, and on that basis, he argues that every religion in existence today was at first, at its base, nothing but this Dīn which the Qur'ān speaks of, the Dīn delivered through every Prophet and embodied in every scripture. The Shar'a or the law or the code of conduct, he points out, has varied, as warranted by the exigencies of time and conditions of life prevailing at different times among different sections of mankind. The Quranic recommendation is therefore not to wrangle over these variations, so long as they do not belie the basic ideology. What should primarily matter is the ideology, the Dīn, a firm belief in the Unity of God expressing itself in righteous action such as shall operate for the unity of man.

Mawlana Azad's painful observation is that this ideology which was meant to keep mankind together as but one family, has, in the course of history, been disfigured by vested interests giving rise to a variety of credal dissensions between man and man. He devotes one full section to the subject of the concept of God to show how the followers of each religion including Islam have interfered with the basic concept of Divine Unity. It is round this primary regret of his that his entire discourse revolves : and he makes a pathetic appeal to one and all to return to the basic ideology. This is the way to peace and harmony among mankind. It is, in fact, a call for religious tolerance and self-purification.

It is a matter for regret that the entire body of Mawlana's Quranic studies has so far remained out of the reach of the educated classes not conversant with the Urdu language. Had a simultaneous attempt been made from the beginning, even from the days of the first appearance of his Al-Hilal, to transmit the result of his research in the field of Quranic interpretation at least into English, the language generally known to the higher intelligentzia in most countries, I dare say a powerful stimulus might have been furnished to the thoughtful mind everywhere to revive the universal element in every religion, as recommended by the Qur'ān, to function as a force for religious tolerance and world unity.

Still, a beginning may yet be made in this direction. Of all the writings of Mawlana Azad, the Tarjumān-al-Qur'ān is his magnum opus, and the opening section of it serving as a commentary of the Sūrat-ul-Fātiḥa is a masterly introduction to the study of the Qur'ān. So great is the importance attached by the Mawlana to this opening chapter, that in explaining the ideology that it outlines, he has surveyed the entire Qur'ān. Regular students of the Qur'ān will find therein a store of Quranic knowledge such as is not found in current commentaries. For their benefit, the entire commentary of the Sūrat-ul-Fātiḥa has, at the instance of Mawlana Azad himself, been rendered into English by the present writer. This will be issued separately. But for others, who may desire to have a general view of the ideology presented therein, an analytical summary of it is attempted in the following pages, divided into several chapters as sug-gested by the leading concepts which it embodies.

In presenting the subject, the writer has ventured to reproduce the very manner of Mawlana's exposition by transplanting into the resume appropriate passages from the original as translated into English, so much so, that the resume may be regarded as a summary of his views in his own style and language. When the third volume of the Tarjumān-ul-Qur'ān is published, it will be possible for scholars, better equipped than the present writer, to appraise at their full value the acute genius of this great savant of India, and the service he has rendered not only to Islamic learning, but to world thought. Till then, the present attempt at portrayal, inadequate as it is, may serve as a preliminary introduction.*

My thanks are due to Dr. M. Rahatullah Khan, M.A., D.Phil. (Leipzig), Curator, State Central Library, Hyderabad, for having very kindly prepared the index to this volume, and read the proofs while its matter was in the press.

SYED ABDUL LATIF.

* The Preface as it ends here had the benefit of Mawlana Azad's perusal even as the text of this volume and is printed in the form in which it was received back from him for transmission to the press.—S.A.L.

CONTENTS

CHAPTER I

THE QURANIC VIEW OF GOD

In the study of a religion, the aspect of it which calls for primary consideration is the concept of Divinity which it presents; for, in the last analysis, it is this which furnishes the measure of its worth or of its value to life.

The idea of God has had a chequered history. One may, on the analogy of matter, be tempted to read an evolutionary process underlying its formation. But strange as it may seem, a reverse process is what has been at work. The belief in the existence of God, points out Mawlana Azad, was never the achievement of the human mind, so that one might care to trace its development upward. It is ingrained in the human nature. The Quranic contention is that the very first vision which man had of God was of God's oneness or Unity, the vision of an unseen almighty being who must have created all that he could see or feel about and around him, and that this vision slowly underwent a change marking a sort of retrogression and giving rise to the concept of multiplicity or polytheism. In other words, instead of evolution, a backward movement manifests itself in the history of theism. It is only in the field of attributes, however, that the theory of evolution may afford valuable help in investigation.

The urge among European scholars to treat monotheism as the result of an evolutionary process had its rise about the close of the 18th century. But it was during the second half of the 19th century that most of the theories upholding the idea were formulated.* Attempts were made to locate the origin of the belief in God severally in nature myths, fetish worship, worship of ancestors, primitive animism, astral and nature mythology, necromancy and so forth. The idea which the different theories nursed was that even as every other phenomenon in life, monotheism was the result of an evolutionary process.

The revolutionary disclosures of the 20th century, however, soon gave a powerful set-back to this idea. Researches carried on among the wild tribes of South East Australia and of some of the islands of the Pacific Ocean, as also among the primitive tribes of North America who from time immemorial have observed the most primitive forms of life marked by a total absence of every sign of evolutionary growth in their cultural aspect, together with researches in Egyptology, and the excavations carried on in Iraq and Mohenjadaro, all show that the belief in an ultimate ground of things was not the result of any evolutionary process. The latest Semetic studies also lend support to this view. They disclose that all the Semetic tribes originally believed in an unseen Supreme Being. The archaeological finds discovered after the First World War in the valley of 'Aqaba in Hejaz and in the terrain of Shamar in Northern Syria go to emphasise further this fact of history. In short, the 20th century investigations have all gone to establish that the earliest belief which inspired man was a belief in the unity of God.

It seems that when the world opened out before man in the very first stage of his history, he was impelled by

* Mawlana Azad gives here in his original an account of the leading theories. Vide pp. 124 to 130. Tarjumān-al-Qur'ān, Vol. I, Second Edition, Lahore, 1947.

his very nature and the situation in which he found himself to believe in the existence of an Almighty Being who must have created all that he beheld around him. It was only in subsequent stages that he began to body forth for this Almighty Being qualities or attributes as suggested themselves to him on the analogy of his own qualities. It was thus that his initial belief in God took a retrogressive turn. As Mawlana Azad puts it: Adam was created with light within, but his progeny frittered it away and let in darkness instead. This is borne out by the ancient traditions of Egypt, Greece, Chaldea, India, China and Iran. They reveal the fact that man at first lived a life guided by Nature. Indeed, the Old Testament definitely assigns to Adam a heavenly existence. It is only when he falls into error that he is deprived of it. Light comes first and darkness afterwards. Such is the statement of the Qur'ān:

> Men were at first of one religion only:
> Then they fell to variance.
>
> (Q. 10: 19)

> Mankind were of one religion, and God sent prophets as comforters and warners and He sent down with them the word of Truth that it might decide the disputes of men.
>
> (Q. 2: 213)

The differences which have marked the course of religion, points out Mawlana Azad, have mostly been in respect of the attributes of God, and not in respect of the existence of God. The intellect of man is bounded by his senses. Its perception does not ordinarily cross their frontiers, and it cannot therefore easily comprehend the Absolute. Whenever he tries to visualize a thing unseen, he invariably conjures up for it qualities of which he is aware in his own person. In the beginning, his mind was, so to say, in the infant stage. The picture of divine attributes, raised in his mind, necessarily partook of his intellectual infancy. But as his mind developed with the advance of time, the picture too of God began to undergo a corresponding change; so much so, that the higher the qualities that he displayed in his own life, the higher were the attributes with which he invested his God. It is from this standpoint that an evolutionary process may be traced in the human approach to divine attributes. Mawlana Azad notices three distinct strains in the process which dovetail, one into another, marking a move from anthropomorphism and anthropophuism to transcendentalism, from polytheism back to monotheism, and from the vision of a God of awe and terror to that of a God of love.

The question here arises: Why was the initial concept of man in respect of God one of awe and terror? The answer is clear. The constructive beauty of the Universe lay concealed under the shroud of destructiveness. In the infant stage of his intellect, man could not catch the hidden beauty. He was frightened by the splitting which precedes construction and could not catch the beauty of the things to shape. For this, one needs insight or inward vision, and this came to him in gradual measure as time went on.

Hence it is that when the mind of man began at first to dwell on the attributes of God, it was more easily influenced by the destructive aspect of Nature than by its constructiveness. Thunder and lightning in the clouds, volcanic eruptions in the mountains, earthquakes, river floods, and storms in the ocean—all these disturbing phenomena created awe and terror in him, and he began to visualize his God as the God of terror. He could not see the God of beauty in the frightening thunder and lightning or in the molten lava flowing from volcanoes.

The early conditions also in which man lived were not such as could dispel his feeling of awe and terror. He felt he was weak and unprotected. He looked upon everything else beside him as something inimical to him and intent on his destruction. The hosts of mosquitoes from marshes hovered around him ; poisonous creepers met him at every turn ; and wild animals threatened him wherever he went. The burning sun above, and the shifting seasons of the year looked to him, at first, as hostile to his well-being. Every thing seemed to him designed to frighten him and overawe. The God that he conjured up for himself was therefore one of terror. But as time passed, a gradual change came over him, as also in his environment. His sense of despair was now mixed with the sense of hope, so much so, that in his concept of God, an equal place was given to the attributes of grace and beauty alongside of the old concept of awe and terror. The new awakening manifested itself in the deification also of the forces of benevolence dispensing food, wealth, beauty and knowledge. The mythology of Greece has no doubt a fascination of its own. But even there, the early entrants in the Greek pantheon were the gods of terror. In India, even till this day, the gods of destruction out-number those of grace and benevolence.

Prior to the delivery of the Qur'ān, the highest that the human intellect could achieve was to think of God without any symbolic aid. But, in respect of divine attributes, no concept anywhere could invest God with any attributes other than the human. Even the Judaic concept which disallowed image-worship in any form was not free from the taint of similitude. The mind of man had not risen high enough to discard the veils of anthropomorphic similitudes and directly behold the splendour of divine attributes.[1] Even Christ when he desired to speak of the universal mercy of God was obliged to employ the similitude of relationship subsisting between father and son—a similitude which through an inept approach to the meaning and illustrative purpose of Christ went to stimulate eventually among his followers the urge to instal him into the position of a veritable son of God, and indeed of God Himself.

The peculiarity of the Qur'ān is that it lifts the veils of anthropomorphic similitudes from across the vision of God and allows us to take a transcendental view of Him in His attributes.

> Nought is there like Him.
>
> (Q. 41 : 11)
>
> No vision taketh Him in,
> But he taketh in all vision.
>
> (Q. 6: 104)
>
> Say : He is God, the One only :
> God, on whom all depend !
> He begetteth not, nor is he begotten ;
> And there is none like Him.
>
> (Q. 112: 1-4)

Prior to the advent of the Qur'ān, two ways had been followed to catch a glimpse of Reality. One was to invest the Absolute with attributes, the other was to divest Him of all attributes. The former process led to anthropomorphism and obstructed the perception of Reality.

* In an illuminating lengthy discourse, Mawlana Azad surveys the concepts of God in relation to attributes held by the leading religions of the world at the advent of Islam—pp. 135 to 165, *Tarjumān-al-Qur'ān*, Vol. I, Second Edition, Lahore 1947.

The other process was what was particularly followed by the Upanișads : It was a process of negations—'Nēti, Nēti'. Such a process undoubtedly affords a very advanced view of transcendentalism ; but it ends in nullification, and denies us the consolation of positive belief. At best it can promote a philosophic outlook, but can never become an active or living faith. It was to prevent the process of negations from reaching its logical destiny that a process of retraction had to be devised. The Absolute Brahmān had therefore to descend into the concrete form of Īșwara to avoid total nullity.

Such were the two alternatives to choose between. The Qur'ān avoids both the extremes and follows a line of its own. It pursues a path along which we not only get a transcendental vision of God, but feel competent to dispel the anthropomorphic atmosphere that may attempt to close round it. It affirms individual attributes, one by one ; but it prevents each attribute developing any anthropomorphic touch. 'He is the Living, the Almighty, the Creator, the Merciful, the All Seeing, the All Hearing, the All Knowing', and so forth. Not merely this, the Qur'ān employs here and there, without any hesitation, every form of figurative expression admissible in literature. But it makes it clear that nothing may be compared to God. His living is not like our living ; His seeing or hearing or knowing is not like ours. The metaphor of hand may be used to denote His power and forgiveness, and that of '*Arsh* or Throne to denote His Majesty and His All-Embracing control of the Universe. But the sense is not the same as may be formed of these in our mind in relation to human activity.

The attitude adopted by the Qur'ān is the only way

out. On the one hand, Reality is so high that the human intellect feels helpless to scale up to it. On the other, the restless urge in human nature to have a vision of this Reality is genuine enough. If we lean wholly toward transcendentalism, we end in negation. If we go headlong in the affirmation of attributes, we run the risk of falling into the lap of anthropomorphism. The Qur'ān therefore neither gives the reins to transcendentalism, nor lets affirmation of attributes degenerate into anthropomorphism. The attitude is thus clearly distinguishable from the one adopted by the Aryan Philosophy. While the Aryan mind, in its urge to behold Reality, *personified God Himself*, thereby throwing the door open to image-worship, the Qur'ān satisfied this urge by *personifying only the Attributes of God*, and not His Being, allowing, in consequence, absolutely no chance for symbolic representation.

The Quranic concept of the Unity of God is definite, and has both a positive and a negative side to it. The positive side is that God is one and one only. The negative side is that there is none like Him. And when there is none like Him, it follows that whatever attributes that might be assigned to God cannot be assigned at the same time to any other. The former postulate is called 'uniqueness in essence', and the latter 'uniqueness in attributes'. Prior to the emergence of the Quranic concept, stress was laid more on the uniqueness of God in His essence than on His uniqueness in attributes. It is why we find in every earlier religion the belief in the Unity of God expressing itself in or subsisting side by side with image and hero worship.

In India, probably from the very beginning, it was tacitly admitted that hero-worship and the worship of demigods were indispensable for the masses, reserving the worship of God in His uniqueness or Unity for the elite only. The same was the case in Greece. The Greek thinkers were certainly not unaware of the fact that the gods of Olympus had no reality about them. Still, save Socrates, few had felt the need for interfering in the people's belief in demigods. The fear was that if that belief was not maintained, the socio-religious life of the people would disintegrate.

In this connection, the aspect which calls for special attention is the status accorded to the founder of a religion. True that no teaching can acquire the reputation of greatness, so long as the personality of the teacher does not itself display the quality of greatness. But there is a limit to greatness of personality. It is here that many have stumbled, because they could not draw the boundary line for it. The result was that the founder of a religion or of a school of philosophy was hailed sometimes as an incarnation of God, and sometimes as the son of God ; and where this was not possible, he was, at any rate, offered the honour and devotion usually offered to God.

The Jews, for instance, did, no doubt, not take to image-worship. They nevertheless did erect in the course of their history statues over the remains of their prophets and endow them with a halo of holiness usually associated with objects of worship. There is absolutely no room for image-worship in the teaching of Buddha. In fact, his last testament which has reached us was: 'See that you do not worship my ashes. If you do, the path of salvation will be closed to you.' But what his followers actually did is all before us. They not only erected places of worship over Buddha's ashes and relics, but as means of propagation of his religion, installed images of him throughout the world. The fact is that a larger number of images of Buddha exist today in the world than of any other personality or deity. Likewise, the teaching of Christianity originally concentrated on the Unity of God; but within one hundred years of its advent, Christ himself was raised to the position of God. On the other hand, the Qur'ān laid so great an emphasis on the Unity of God both in His essence and attributes that it blocked for ever all avenues for polytheism and like abberations. It is this which constitutes its principal contribution to the concept of God.

The Qur'ān asserts that God alone is worthy of worship. If you turn to any other in devotion, you cease to be a believer in the Unity of God. It says that He it is who answers the cry of man and fulfils his prayers. So, if you associate any other with Him in your prayers, you simply associate that other in the divinity or attributes also of God. Indeed, your belief itself in the Unity of God gets tainted. It is why in the *Sūrat-ul-Fātiḥa*, the form of prayer is set: '*Thee* alone do we serve and from *Thee* alone do we seek aid.' The emphasis is on *Thee alone*. Such great stress does the Qur'ān lay on the uniqueness of God both in His essence and His attributes that there is hardly a page in the whole of the Qur'ān where the truth is not pointedly brought to view.

The stress becomes intelligible when we proceed to appraise the position assigned by the Qur'ān to the Prophet of Islam. Over and over again does it point out that the prophet of Islam is but a human being and a servant of God. The very basic belief in Islam runs: 'I affirm that there is no God except Allāh, and I affirm that Muhammad is his servant and his message-bearer.' In this formula, the affirmation of the unity of God is as emphatic as the affirmation of the position of the prophet as but a servant of God and the bearer of His message. Why was this made the basic doctrine of Islam? It was done simply to prevent the prophet from ever being hailed as God or as His incarnation, or invested with the attributes and honour exclusive to God. No one can enter the fold of Islam who does not subscribe to the belief that the Prophet is but a servant of God, even as he subscribes to the belief in the Unity of God.

That was the reason why, notwithstanding the numerous dissensions which arose among Muslims after the death of the Prophet, no difference was entertained among them on the question of his personality. Not many hours had passed since the Prophet's death, when Abū Bakr, the prophet's father-in-law and the first Khalif of Islam, ascending the pulpit proclaimed:

> 'He who worshipped Muhammad, let him know that Muhammad is dead; and he who worshipped God, let him know that God lives always. He never dies.'

Prior to the advent of the Qur'ān, distinction was made between the common people and the elite in the imparting of religious knowledge. In India, three grades were fixed. For the common people, image-worship was prescribed, and for the elite, the method of communion with God, while for the elite of the elite, the privilege of pantheistic experience. The same was the case in Greece. It was considered that the concept of an abstract deity was possible only for those who were versed in philosophic lore and that it was safe for the common people to engage themselves in the worship of demigods only. The Qur'ān brushed aside this distinction. It presented for one and all but a single way of approach to God and afforded to them but a single view of divine attributes. It held before both, the philosopher or gnostic and the unlettered shepherd or rustic, but one and the same glow of Reality. It opened for one and all but one door of faith and inward peace.

An aspect of this subject here calls for consideration. The distinction which was observed in India between the common people and the elite was the result of the practical sense of compromise which prevailed here. Here, every form of religious belief or exercise was given a home, and every thought, the freedom to grow and develop. Religious differences which among other nations led to internecine civil wars were regarded here as but subjects of compromise. Adjustability was the spirit of life here. A Vedantist knows that communion with Reality is infinitely higher than image-worship. But he never sets his face against image-worship; for, he thinks that this is the first stage in the journey to God, and that whatever path one may choose to traverse, the ultimate goal for one and all is one and the same.

The spirit of tolerance which has characterised Indian history, no doubt, deserves a meed of praise. But life is an expression of action and inter-action, and unless we draw a limit or line for every type of activity, canons of knowledge and morality will get disturbed, and we shall cease to possess any definite sense of moral values. Tolerance is a good thing, but strength of belief and opinion, and integrity of thought are also factors of life which we cannot ignore. A line of demarcation for the expression of each quality in us needs to be drawn. For, otherwise, moral injunctions cannot be implemented properly. Once these lines are disturbed or weakened, the edifice of morality begins to totter. Forgiveness for instance, is a good and a beautiful idea. But this very forgiveness, once it over-steps its legitimate boundary, ceases to be forgiveness: it becomes timidity or cowardice. Courage is the highest human quality, but this very quality, once it develops excess, no longer remains courage; it becomes tyranny and oppression.

Here are two situations. You cannot deal with them in the same way. One situation is this. The light of a certain line of faith or of a certain mode of action has dawned on us, and we have come to hold a definite opinion about it. The question arises: what should be our line of action in respect of it? Shall we waver or remain firm in our attitude? The other situation is this. Others, even like us, have reached certain definite conclusions about one and the same thing, and adopt a different way of life from our own. What should be our attitude towards them? Have they or have they not the right to go their own way? Tolerance is to acknowledge the right of another to hold to his own views and follow his own way. Even when his way is clearly the wrong way, you cannot deny him the right to pursue it. But if tolerance is given the latitude to water down your own beliefs and affect your decisions, then, it ceases to be tolerance.

Compromise is a necessity of life. Our life itself is one long compromise. But there should be a limit to it. A line will have to be drawn somewhere, in order to feel secure in the beliefs one cherishes. So long as you do not feel the inward urge to alter that belief, you are bound by it and have the right to cling to it. You will certainly respect the beliefs of others, but you will insist on your right not to let your own belief weaken on that account.

How often has havoc been wrought in the field of belief and action by a disregard of this distinction. Intensity of belief has at times so much obsessed people that all considerations of tolerance have been set aside, and the beliefs and ways of life of others forcibly invaded. At times also, tolerance has been given so great a latitude that strength of belief has ceased to bear any meaning. Examples of the former may easily be furnished from the history of religious persecutions, and those of the latter from the history of India. Here in India, the highest flights of the human mind could not remain immune from the touch of superstition. The process has gone on of compromise between knowledge and intellect, on the one hand, and ignorance and superstition, on the other. The beauty of the Indian mind and all its great mental achievements have thus been seriously affected by superstition and image-worship. The findings of the present-day historians of India are all to this effect. The distinguished Hindu scholar, Dr. Radhakrishnan, while reviewing the impact of the non-Aryan culture of India on the culture of the Aryan settlers here observes :

> 'The explanation of the miscellaneous character of the Hindu religion, which embraces all the intermediate regions of thought and belief from the wandering fancies of savage superstitions to the highest insight of daring thought, is here. From the beginning, the Aryan religion was expansive, self-developing and tolerant. It went on accommodating itself to the new forces it met within its growth. In this, can be discerned a refined sense of true humility and sympathetic understanding. The Indian refused to ignore the lower religions and fight them out of existence. He did not possess the pride of the fanatic that his was the one true religion. If a god satisfies the human mind in its own way, it is a form of truth. None can lay hold upon the whole of truth. It can be won only

by degrees, partially and provisionally. But they forgot that intolerance was sometimes a virtue. There is such a thing as Gresham's law in religious matters also. When the Aryan and the Non-Aryan religions, one refined and the other vulgar, the one good and the other base, met, there was the tendency for the bad to beat the good out of circulation.'*

The peculiarity of the Qur'ān is that it refuses to enter into any compromises in the field of beliefs. In its unitary and transcendental concept of God, it is definite and inelastic. This rigidity however, does not prevent it from observing tolerance towards other beliefs. But it certainly refuses to enter into compromises with them.

The Qur'ān bases its concept of God on the inherent universal urges of human nature. It has not made of this concept a riddle which only a special class of intellect alone can solve. What is the universal human feeling about life ? It is that this Universe has not come into being by itself; it has been created : and so, it must have a Creator. What the Qur'ān points out is only this much. Anything over and above this which it deals with does not enter into the doctrinal belief. All that is left to be thought over by man individually, or to be experienced personally.

> And whoso maketh efforts for us, in our
> ways will we guide them.
>
> (Q. 29 : 69)

> On Earth are signs for men of firm
> belief, and also in your own selves :
> Will ye not then behold them ?
>
> (Q. 51 : 20-21)

* 'Indian Philosophy' by Dr. Radhakrishnan, Vol. I, p. 119, Second Edition.

Here comes in the peculiar distinction which Islam observes between the masses and the elite. The Hindu thinkers distributed different grades of thought among different classes of society. From the standpoint of knowledge and belief, Islam makes no such distinction. It offers to every human being one and the same knowledge in respect of Reality. But aptitudes differ. Not everyone feels the same thirst for knowledge. People as a class might have certain dispositions ; but individuals among them possess varying aptitudes for knowledge. According to the extent of one's aptitude, each is left free to make his advance. An authentic tradition of the Prophet is related by Bukhāri and Muslim which speaks of three grades of minds—*Islām*, *Imān* and *Iḥsān*. *Islām* consists in the affirmation of the Islamic doctrinal beliefs, in the observance of daily prayers, in the performance of Haj or pilgrimage to the Ka'aba whenever found convenient during one's life-time, in the observance of fast in the month of Ramaḍān, and in the payment of Zakāt or the poor-due. *Imān* lies not only in the affirmation of the doctrinal beliefs, but in entertaining an absolute conviction about them. And *Iḥsān* is a state of mind to which the following advice of the Prophet may aptly apply : ' Pray as if thou seest thy God before thee ; and if thou seest Him not, pray in the conviction that God is, at any rate, seeing you.'

The first stage indicates the general attitude. He who affirms the doctrinal beliefs and discharges certain duties, he has entered the fold of Islam. But mere entry does not argue a state of conviction in him. The first stage of Islam represents only its outward aspect, the elementary side of it. The Second stage is that of *Imān*, where Islam takes hold of one's mind and heart. Once this stage is reached, one enters the circle of the elect. But the matter does not end here. The knowledge of Reality or 'real conviction' comes at a later stage—the stage of *Iḥsān.* But this is not a stage of mere belief or of conviction to be reached by communities as communities or on the group plane. This is the stage of individual experience or of personal illumination. Mere doctrinal belief or intellectual speculation does not promote the growth of this stage. It is not a matter either to teach or to learn. It is the result of personal spiritual endeavour. He who has reached this stage, if he could ever say anything about it, he can say nothing but this: 'Become one like me, and then behold what you can behold.' Says a poet:

> 'Someone asked me: what is love?
> Said I: Become one like me, and
> then you will know what it is.'

Islam has made provision for the satisfaction of every kind of spiritual thirst. For an average man, there is the initial stage; for the more advanced, the second stage; and for the elite, the third. But the thirst is to be quenched at one and the same tavern, although the cup for each may be different. Each gets the cup that befits him.

> 'The Saqi pours wine to every one from the same jar;
> But every one reacts
> According to his talents.'

It may be mentioned here that Muslim philosophers, particularly the Ṣūfis, have evolved a theory in respect of God, popularly known as the theory of Waḥdat-al-Wajūd; or of 'Unity of Being'. It has been prompted by certain expressions in the Qur'ān, such as, 'God is the First and the Last; the Apparent and the Hidden';

'Wherever ye turn, ye will behold the countenance of God'; 'He is nearer to you than your jugular vein'; 'Every moment He discloses Himself in fresh glory'; and 'All shall return to God', and so on. Indeed, Shah Waliullāh, the famous Muslim theologian of Delhi, goes to the extent of asserting: 'If I wish to prove the theory of the "Unity of Being", I can do so by a reference to the very text of the Qur'ān and Ḥadith.' But the plain fact, cautions Mawlana Azad, should not be lost sight of that it will not be proper to give to these expressions any far-fetched interpretation, or invest them with a meaning or significance which the Muslims of the Prophet's time did not attach. As for the rest, says he, the perception of God through illumination which gnostics enjoy is certainly not in conflict with the principles of the Qur'ānic concept of God. The Qur'ānic concept is comprehensive enough to accommodate every unitary concept of God. Those who have reached the stage of *Iḥsān*, says he, can see Reality even in its hidden glories, and scale the highest spiritual heights possible for the human soul.

CHAPTER II

THE ATTRIBUTE OF PROVIDENCE

In dealing with the attributes of God, Mawlana Azad makes a general observation. He says that the unity of God, in its relation to the order of life at work in the Universe expresses itself in an unity of attributes. In other words, the attributes of God do not operate in individual isolation but blend one into every other so as to produce harmony in life. Of these, the *Sūrat-ul-Fātiha* or the opening chapter of the Qur'ān, refers to the basic among them, viz., the attributes of Providence, Graciousness or Mercy, Justice, and Guidance or Revelation. He discusses these seriatim in his commentary, and surveys the entire Qur'ān for their exposition. He begins with the very first attribute of God which attracts the attention of the Qur'ān, the attribute of Divine Providence or Rubūbiyat.

The term 'Rubūbiyat' is derived from 'Rabb which is a common root for several words in the Semitic languages. In Hebrew, Syriac and Arabic, the term 'Rabb' means nourisher or one who provides the means of sustenance. Since the need for nourishment is of the basic needs of human life, the meaning given to the term 'Rabb' as nourisher may be regarded as but a natural first approach to God which the early Semitic mind could conceive of. The term means also teacher, master, lord, or God. In the Quranic context, the term is invested with a connotation so wide that in the opinion of some of the leading lexicographers, 'Rubūbiyat' means:

> 'To develop a thing from stage to stage, in accordance with its inherent aptitudes and needs, in order that it might attain its full stature or perfection.'

'Rubūbiyat' is thus a process of nourishment providing a thing from moment to moment and from stage to stage all that it needs to gain its fullest possible development. But in the Quranic concept of it, points out Mawlana Azad, this process is always marked by a touch of tenderness. He makes his meaning clear by citing an illustration.

When a child is born, says he, it is but an active lump of flesh displaying an urge for living and calling for nourishment and direction. There then begins a lengthy process of love and affection on the part of the mother, of tender and timely care and unsolicited favours. And this goes on even till it develops into adolescence, both of body and mind. During this period arise needs, not one or two, but numerous which have to be attended to. These vary or change from stage to stage, demanding according to the nature of each stage the requisite love and care and amenities of life. The wisdom of God has instilled into the mind of the mother the quality of 'Rubūbiyat' whereby she looks after the child from the day of its appearance till it enters on the stage of adolescence. When the stomach of the child cannot relish anything except milk, only milk is given. When it can bear stronger diet, such diet is provided. So long as the child cannot stand on its legs, the mother carries it in her lap wherever she goes. When it develops the ability to stand, she holds its finger and helps it take steps one by one.

'Rubūbiyat' is thus a continuous process of providing one with all that one needs in every situation and at every stage. The view which the Qur'ān presents of God as 'Rabb' may now be easily grasped. 'Rabbul 'Ālamin' is the attribute which the Qur'ān applies to God in His role of 'Rabb'. It points out in a striking manner that God is not the 'Rabb' or Nourisher of any particular community or class, but that He is the 'Rabb' of all mankind, and of everything that subsists in the Universe.

System of Providence

Mawlana Azad asserts that the function of Divine 'Rubūbiyat' is discharged under a definite plan. Every thing is furnished with all that its particular nature demands for its existence in every changing situation. Ants crawl on earth, worms push their way in mud and dirt, fish swim in water, birds fly in air, flowers blossom in gardens, elephants wander in the jungle, and stars revolve in the heavens. But on every one of these, rests the protecting eye of Providence, and there is none that is denied its blessings. Indeed, there are countless varieties of creation so infinitisimally small in form that our naked eye cannot perceive them. For them also, the Rubūbiyat of God has made the requisite provision for sustenance and growth with as much care as is bestowed on the bulky elephant. All this, man can observe in his external world. Should he look within himself, he will notice that his life, at every moment of its existence, discloses a world of activity propelled by the Rubūbiyat of God.

> On Earth are signs for men of firm belief;
> And also in your own selves.
> Will ye not then behold them? (Q. 51 : 20-21)

The Outward Aspect

The Qur'ān makes distinction between the creation of the provisions of life and the function of 'Rubūbiyat'. Forces and things there are which in their varied form are of value to the growth and sustenance of life. But the mere provision of them cannot be regarded as an act of 'Rubūbiyat'. That is an expression of creative activity. On the other hand, 'Rubūbiyat' lies in the method and manner of providing these or the system into which they are made to fit. For instance, life needs for its sustenance water and humidity. The presence of water by itself will have no direct significance to life, unless that water is available to life in a particular quantity at a particular time. The creation of water, according to the Qur'ān, is an expression of 'Raḥmat' or divine graciousness, whereas it is His 'Rubūbiyat' which lets this water come down to earth drop by drop and reach every corner of it only in particular seasons and in particular quantity, and search out and quench even the tiniest particle thirsting for water.

> 'And We send down water from the heavens in its due degree and We cause it to settle on the earth, and we have power for its withdrawal too— And by it, We cause gardens of palm trees and vineyards to spring forth for you, in which ye have plenteous fruits, and whereof ye eat.'
>
> (Q. 23 : 18-19)

The Qur'ān often refers to the value of the good things of life and of the measure of each as measured out to every living object, and thus points to the fact of life that Nature provides everything in a particular measure and this under a particular plan.

'And no one thing is there, but with
Us are its store-houses; and We send it not but in settled measure.'

(Q. 15: 21)

'With Him everything is by measure.'

(Q. 13: 8)

'All things We have created after a fixed degree.'

(Q. 54: 49)

Mark! There is water on earth, but that is distributed in a particular manner. Why so? Why do the rays of the Sun raise from the surface of the ocean sheets after sheets of water into the air, and why do the winds shake them so as to let them come down to earth in drops, and that in a particular season? Again, why is it that whenever it rains, it does so in a manner that while a portion of it runs down the surface of the earth, a portion soaks into the earth to a particular depth? Why is snow formed on the top of mountains in a particular season, and why does it melt in another and flow down the mountains to form into rivers meandering over the plains, and watering extensive areas of the earth?

Why should all this happen in a particular form and not in any other? The Qur'ān gives the reply. The Providence of God is at work in Nature, and its purpose is to produce water in this particular fashion and arrange its distribution in this particular way. It is the 'Raḥmat' or the graciousness of God which produces water, but it is His Rubūbiyat or His attribute of Providence which utilizes this water so as to give to every living object its means of sustenance.

'And one of His signs is that He sendeth the wind with glad tidings of rain, both that He may cause you to taste His mercy, and that ships may sail at His command, that out of His bounties ye may seek wealth and that haply ye may render thanks.'

(Q. 30: 46)

The things most needed in life are the things most profusely provided, and similarly, those needed in particular climes or in only particular situations are given local habitation and are limited in quantity. The thing primarily needed is air, for, one can forego food and water for a while, but can hardly live without air. Its provision therefore is so common and plentiful that there is hardly a corner of the earth from where it is absent at any moment. Next in importance is water, which next to air is the largest provision. In every part of the world rivers roam about on the surface, and underneath the ground currents of water keep flowing. In addition, the atmospheric forces are at work to drag water out from the saltish ocean and sweeten it and store it in the air only to return it to the earth whenever it needs it. Next to air and water comes the need for food, and that is spread out in bounteous plenty over the entire globe, and there is not a species of creation which is not provided close to it with its means of sustenance.

If one should ponder over this system of universal Providence, it will be clear to him that this system is devised to sustain life and develop every inherent capacity therein. The Sun is there to give light and heat and methodically draw out water from the ocean. The winds are there to produce alternately coolness and warmth. Sometimes they waft particles of water up into the skies and spread them into layers of vapoury clouds; sometimes they reduce these clouds into water again, and bring it down. The earth is there to serve as a perennial store-house of the means of growth and sustenance, and to offer from within its bosom life to every grain, and growth to every plant. In short, Life's workshop is incessantly engaged in this process. Every force is displaying its talent, and every cause is producing its effect. The moment a thing develops the talent to grow, the entire mechanism of life turns its attention to it. The phenomenal activities of the Sun, the cycle of seasons in all their moods, the forces of the earth, and the inter-action of elements seem intent on seeing that the egg of an ant delivers its offspring and the peasant's bag drops its grain.

> 'And He Hath subjected to you all that there is in the Heavens and all that there is in the Earth: All is from Him.
> Verily, herein are signs for those who reflect.'
>
> (Q. 45: 13)

The strangest thing about this working of Rubūbiyat or Providence, points out Mawlana Azad, is its methodical uniformity, so much so, that a single principle seems to be at work in all things. The stone may appear different from the fragrant flower, but the two receive their sustenance in the same way and are granted growth in the same style. The child of a human being and the twig of a plant may look like belonging to two different orders; but if you look into the way in which they grow and develop, you will find that a single system of life and growth binds them together. Whether it is a slab of stone, a bud of flower, a human child, or an egg of an ant, every one has its time of emergence, of its birth; and the means of sustenance for one and all are provided in advance ere they emerge into life. And then follow for everything, so to say, the stages of childhood, youth, adolescence, manhood, maturity and obsolescence. The principle of growth and decadence, of rise and fall in life, is common to one and all.

> 'It is God who hath created you in weakness: Then after weakness hath given you strength: Then after strength weakness and grey hairs.'
>
> (Q. 30: 54)

> 'Seest thou not that God sendeth down water from heaven, and guideth it along so as to form springs in the earth, then bringeth forth by it corn of varied sorts, then causeth it to wither, and thou seest it become yellow, then crumbleth it away? Lo! herein is instruction for men of insight?'
>
> (Q. 39: 21)

Look at the provision of food. Among the animal-kind there are some animals whose young ones feed on milk, while others feed on a variety of food-stuffs. Ponder over the system of nourishment devised for them. Take the case of man. The moment he takes his birth, the food that he needs provides itself for him in the exact form that his condition demands, and is provided very close to him. The mother, in the intensity of her affection for the new-born babe, hugs him to her bosom, and at that very place, the child finds the store-house of his nourishment. And then look at the manner whereby his graded needs are attended to, calling for a continuous variation in diet. It has to agree with the successive changes in his condition. In the beginning, the stomach of a child is so tender that a highly diluted form of milk is needed for him. That is why the milk of the mother, even as among other animals, is very thin to begin with. But as the child grows and his stomach becomes stronger as time passes, the milk of the mother gradually thickens ; so much so, that as soon as the stage of infancy is over and his stomach develops the capacity to digest the normal food, the breasts of the mother dry up. This is the sign of Providence indicating that the child should no longer depend upon milk, but should be able to try other forms of food.

> 'With pain his mother beareth him ; with pain she bringeth him forth : and his bearing and his weaning is thirty months.'
>
> (Q. 46 : 15)

Again, ponder over the way in which the principle of Providence has ingrained in the very nature of the mother the love that she has to bear towards her child. It is this love of the mother which inspires in her the noblest of sentiments. For her child's sake, there is no sacrifice too great for her to bear. But as the child grows in years, the love of the mother for the child gradually diminishes in intensity and a time comes when, though this feeling does not completely die out as among the lower animals, there is a distinct subsidence in its warmth. Why should it be so ? Why is it that the moment a child is born, this great feeling of love takes a sudden rise in the mother, and why, having lasted for sometime, it gradually disappears ? This is so because such is the working of the principle of Providence, such the condition of its existence. Providence desires that the child in its helpless state should be nourished by others. It has therefore fixed the feeling of love in the mother as a motive force for the child's nourishment. When the child has reached a stage where it no longer needs the careful attention of the mother, the need for her love also does not remain. In fact, its continuance will cause unnecessary strain to the mother and also hinder the child's development. It is only at the infant stage that the child needs tender nursing. It is why the love of the mother is intense at such a stage. But as the child advances in years, the need for external aid of every kind lessens. There is no doubt that a mother's love is always alive for her offspring, however old he may grow. But this has only a social value. It is no longer that instinctive care for him such as it was in his infancy.

There is, however, a little difference between the nursing of a human child and that of an offspring of the lower living order. When for instance, a chicken comes out of its shell, its constitution is different from that of the young one who needs to be fed on milk. It is from the very beginning inclined to live on normal or ordinary food, provided there is some one to show it the way. The moment the chicken comes out, it feels the urge to seek out its food, and the mother hen shows how to pick it out. Sometimes it picks out herself for it, softens it within her stomach and when the chicken opens its mouth, it brings it out from within and puts it into its mouth.

The Inward Aspect

Stranger than the outward aspect of this scheme of Providence is the inward aspect of it. Whatever provision one might find in the visible material aspect of life, it will be of no value to it, if each living object were not gifted at the same time with an inward talent to make the right use of the provision afforded. The two are so devised that the forces at work within are endowed with the talent to harmonize with the outward material provisions of life, and help its growth and development. There is no object of creation the constitution of which is repellant to the means of its sustenance.

In this connection, Mawlana Azad brings under consideration two factors of life to which the Qur'ān draws repeated attention. One is what is called 'Taqdīr' loosely rendered into English as fate, the other, 'Hidāyat', or guidance.

Taqdīr—The meaning of 'Taqdīr' is 'to assign' a particular role to everything whether quantitatively or qualitatively. We therefore notice that every object is bound both in its outward and inward aspects by conditions warranted or fixed by its very nature, and that these conditions are in perfect consonance with the variegated demands of its growth and development.

> 'Everything hath He created
> And measured out to each its measure.'
>
> (Q. 25: 2)

The question arises: Why is it that every object takes its rise in an environment most congenial to it or why should every object of creation both in its inward and outward aspects agree with the character of its environment and vice-versa? This is so because, such is the condition of life or 'Taqdīr' fixed for each object in the interests of the object itself by its Wise Creator. The law of 'Taqdīr' is not confined to the animal or mineral world alone, but governs everything. Even the world of planets is bound by it.

> 'The sun rolls on along its prescribed course.
> This, the ordinance of the Mighty, the Knowing.'
>
> (Q. 36: 38)

It is due to this law that every object of creation finds in its environment all that it needs for its sustenance and development. The bird that flies, the fish that swims, the quadruped that walks, or the insect that crawls, has each a body which suits its environment or such as that environment demands. You do not find a bird live in water, because it cannot supply the environment which a bird needs. The fish does not take its rise on the dry land, because dryness is not agreeable to its life. If an object born in a certain environment rushes into another, it comes into conflict with this law of life, the law of 'Taqdīr'. It either ceases to exist, or if it continues to exist at all, it gradually develops a constitution and a disposition which conform to the character and behaviour of its new surroundings. And then each species is moulded to suit a particular environment. An object which takes its rise in a cold climate is meant to thrive only in that climate. The same is true of those that take their rise in hot climates. The bear thriving round the North Pole is not noticeable along the Equator. The animals of the Torrid Zone are not found in the Frigid.

Such is the law of Dispensation in Nature or of Taqdīr. Let us now turn to the other factor viz. Hidāyat.

Hidāyat—'Hidāyat' means to show the way, to give direction along a path, to guide; and there are several forms of this of which mention will be made in detail at a later stage. Here attention is to be drawn only to that primary form of 'Hidāyat' which opens out for every object of creation appropriate avenues of nourishment, and which stimulates its wants and directs it to the means of its satisfaction. This 'Hidāyat' or direction of Nature is indeed the *Hidāyat* of *Rubūbiyat.* Were it not for this Hidāyat implicit in Rubūbiyat, no object of creation will profit by the means of sustenance and growth provided around it, and indeed life itself will cease to function.

This directing force, says the Qur'ān, is nothing but the instinctive urge of nature, or the talent inherent in sense-perception. It is this inward force which actuates a thing to be drawn to its means of sustenance. The offspring of a human being or of an animal, the moment it is delivered from the womb of its mother, instinctively feels that its means of sustenance is in the breasts of its mother and forthwith draws itself to them. The moment it touches the nipple of its mother's breast, it automatically starts the process of sucking. We often see how the kitten, the moment they are delivered, and even before they open their eyes and the mother is still licking at them, rush themselves to the breasts of their mother. The infant which has just come out into life and which has not as yet been affected by its external world, instinctively realizes that the breasts of its mother are the storc-house of its nourishment, and promptly reaches its mouth to them. It is instinct which guides the infant to its nourishment, before it is guided to it by the light of its own sense perception.

If you happen to have a cat in your house, you will notice what she does when she gets pregnant. Suppose this is her first experience. The moment she feels that the time for delivery is approaching, she begins to search for a place of security for her offspring to be. It ransacks every nook and corner of the house for the right place. Once she delivers her offspring in that place, she seems to feel a sort of apprehension for their safety; so much so, that she shifts them from place to place. What is it which impels this cat to search out places of security for her coming offspring, or what is it that gives the idea to her that they would need security? What is that which lets her feel that the moment her offspring come out, their enemy, the he-cat, will be roaming about to sense and hunt them, and that she should change their place of security from moment to moment? Clearly this is the *Hidāyat* of instinct provided in the cat by the Divine *Rubūbiyat*. This instinct is inherent in every living object to open out for it the way to life and its sustenance.

The next stage in this scheme of direction is that of the senses, and of the reasoning faculty. The lower animals, though they do not possess the intellect which helps reasoning and reflection, they have in them the talent of sense perception to the extent they need in their particular spheres of life and by means of which they regulate and satisfy their wants of life—their needs of habitation, food, reproduction, and safety. But this talent in them is not uniform. On the other hand, it is given to each in proportion to the demands of its needs. The sense of smell is very acute in the ant, for, it is through this sense that it has to fetch its food. The sight of the eagle or of the vulture is very keen, for, otherwise it cannot locate its food from on high. It is unnecessary to find out whether this talent in the lower animals exists in them from the very day of their inception, or that it develops in them gradually in response to the demands of their environment. It is enough to know that this talent in them is the gift of Nature.

It must be clear by now that, according to the Qur'ān, the Rubūbiyat of God expresses itself in a comprehensive plan of provision for every object of creation, affording balance (Taswiyah) or proportion to its constitution, a destiny or character appropriate to each (Taqdīr), and an inward and outward sense of direction to it operating for its free movement in life (Hidāyat). Indeed, the Qur'ān takes particular care to make a mention of these provisions. Says it:

> 'Praise the name of Thy Lord, the Most High!
> Who hath created, and balanced *all things*,
> Who hath fixed their destinies and guideth them.'
>
> (Q. 87 : 1-3)

The Underlying purpose—Such is the picture which the Qur'ān presents of the process of Rubūbiyat of God by a reference to the nature of life at work in the Universe. The presentation has a specific purpose to serve and that is to offer the proof or evidence of the Unity of God on the one hand, and to bring home to the mind of man, on the other, that every thing in the Universe is so designed that it is linked to every other under a single principle of life and that everything is fitted into this scheme for a specific purpose and that nothing is created in vain:

> 'God hath created the Heavens and Earth "in truth" or for a serious end:
> Verily, in this is a sign (of Divine purpose) to those who believe.'
>
> (Q. 29 : 43)

> 'Our Lord! All this, Thou hath not created in vain.'
>
> (Q. 3 : 188)

This purposive aspect of creation, Mawlana Azad styles as Takhlīq bil-Ḥaq or creation for a serious end. The term bil-Ḥaq occurs in various places in the Qur'ān just to emphasise that nothing exists without its value to life, and that Nature itself desires that whatever is to be fashioned should be so fashioned that it must contain within it all that it needs for its subsistence.

> 'For a serious end hath He set the heavens and the earth: It is of Him that the night returneth upon the day, and that the day returneth upon the night: and He controlleth the Sun and the Moon so that each speedeth to an appointed goal.'
>
> (Q. 39:7)

> 'It is He who hath appointed the Sun for brightness and the Moon for a light, and hath ordained her stations that ye may learn the numbering of years and the reckoning (of time). God hath not created all this but for a serious end. He maketh his signs clear to those who understand.'
>
> (Q. 10:5)

The same term 'bil-Ḥaq' is also used, to mean beauty of Nature or to suggest that within the bosom of the Universe or through and through its Nature, there is at work a law of beauty or harmony which demands that everything that fashions or shapes itself within it, should be a thing of beauty or perfection:

> 'He hath created the heavens and the earth for a serious end, and hath fashioned you and given goodly forms.'
>
> (Q. 64:3)

In like manner, the Qur'ān cites the law of causation as being implicit in the 'Takhlīq-bil-Ḥaq'. Everything in this world has a talent appropriate to its role in life and which in its manifestation has to produce a specific result. These talents or characteristics and the results which flow from them are immutable. How then can we expect that the good or the evil character of our actions will not produce corresponding results? Can the Law of Nature which discriminates between the good and the evil in everything fail to operate only in the field of human actions?

> 'Deem they whose gettings are only evil, that we will deal with them as with those who believe and work righteousness, so that their lives and deaths shall be alike? Ill do they Judge. In all truth hath God created the heavens and the earth that he may reward every one as he shall have wrought; and they shall not be wronged.'
>
> (Q. 45:20-21)

The 'life hereafter' or the life after death is also a concomitant of the same '*Takhlīq-bil-Ḥaq*'. Everything in the Universe serves a purpose or moves towards a specific goal. So it is with the life of man which has a purpose to serve or a goal towards which it has to move. The goal is the 'life hereafter'. For, it is unthinkable that man should be created just to live for a few moments and then get completely annihilated.

> 'Have they not considered within themselves that God hath not created the heavens and the earth and all that is between them but for a serious end and for a fixed term? But truly most men believe not that they shall meet their Lord.'
>
> (Q. 30:7)

Rububiyat: Proof of Unity of God

It will be interesting to note here that the Qur'ān draws upon the display of divine attributes for its argument in support of its leading doctrinal postulates, particularly on the function of Rubūbiyat. In respect of the unity of God, for instance, its plea is that the very fact that the working of the Universe should regulate itself in such a way that everything therein contributes to life and growth and provides for every situation and every condition, should instinctively raise the conviction in man that there exists a being who provides life to the entire universe and looks after it and who for that purpose must necessarily possess certain attributes, without the display of which such a complete and flawless machinery of existence would never have taken its rise. The Qur'ān asks: Can the instinct of man ever impel him to believe that all this machinery of life has come into existence by itself, and that no aim or purpose underlies it? Is it possible that this machinery of existence, such as it is, has no designer for it whatsoever? Does this entire order of life owe its existence to just a blind and deaf Nature, a lifeless matter, or an insensitive electron, and not to a being possessing a will of its own and a directing intellect?

If so, the position will be this. The function of providence is at work everywhere; and this without an agent behind it. There is design in everything and this without a designer. Mercy is dispensed and this without a merciful dispenser. In short, everything is there and this without there being anything. The nature of man can hardly agree to believe that there can ever be an action without an actor, orderliness without a director, a plan without a planner, a building without a builder, a design without a designer, everything without the existence of anything. The very instinct of man will cry out that such cannot be the case. His very nature is so constituted that it cannot but affirm. It has no room for doubt or disbelief.

The Qur'ān points out that it is against the nature of man that he should ponder over the working of the universe and yet deny the existence of an all-embracing Providence. The Qur'ān says: Man can deny everything under the stress of indifference or arrogance, but he cannot deny his own nature. He can go against everything, but he cannot go against himself. When he looks around and finds that the hand of Providence is at work everywhere, his very nature will proclaim that what he beholds cannot exist without a Providence.

Be it noted that the method of presentation observed by the Qur'ān is not to offer postulates or intellectual poses and to base its argument thereon. On the other hand, its appeal is to man's natural instincts and aptitudes. It points out that the sense of God is inherent in human nature. If one denies it through indifference, he needs to be warned against that indifference. But the method to employ for this should not wholly be intellectual in character. On the other hand, it should be such as could touch his heart and rouse his conscience. Once that is done, he needs no argument to bring conviction to him. That will come to him as a matter of course. It is why the Qur'ān cites man's own nature as an argument against himself.

> 'Nay, man is a telling witness against himself, although he tenders excuses.'
>
> (Q. 75:14-15)

The Qur'ān addresses human nature itself and invites an answer from its very depths.

> 'Say: Who supplieth you sustenance from the heaven and the earth? Who hath power over hearing and sight? And who bringeth forth the living from the dead, and bringeth forth

the dead from the living? And who ruleth over all things? They will surely say: "God". Will ye not therefore mind Him?

Such then is God, your true Lord: and when truth is gone, what remaineth but error? How then are ye so perverted?'

(Q. 10:32-33)

The Qur'ān asks further:

'Is not God the more worthy of the gods they join with Him?

Is not he (the more worthy) who hath made the heavens and the earth, and hath sent down rain to you from the sky by which we cause luxuriant groves to spring up. It is not in your power to cause the trees to grow. What! a god with God? Yea! They are people who ascribe equals (unto Him).

Is not He (the more worthy) who hath set the Earth so firm, and placed rivers in its fold and hath placed mountains upon it and set a barrier between the two seas? What! a God with God? Nay, most of them know not.

Is not He (the more worthy) who answereth the oppressed when they cry to Him, and taketh off their ills, and make you to succeed your sires on the earth? What! a God with God? Little do they reflect!

Is not He (the more wortny) who guideth you in the darkness of the land and of the sea, and who sendeth forth the winds as heralds of His mercy? What! a God with God? Far from God be, the Exalted High, what ye join with Him!

> Is not He (the more worthy) who projects creation, then reneweth it, and who supplieth you out of the heaven and the earth ? What ! a god with God ? Say : Bring forth your proofs, if ye speak the truth.'
>
> (Q. 27:60-65)

Every one of the questions raised here is a definite argument in itself; for, to every one of these questions there is but one answer, and it is that human nature is an universal and recognised factor to reckon with.

The innumerable references made in the Qur'ān to the means of life provided to every object in the universe and to the diverse aspects of the system of providence form in fact the basis of the Quranic argument in support of the Unity of God.

> 'Let man look at his food ;
> It was We who (first) rained down the copious rains,
> Then cleft the earth with clefts,
> And caused the up-growth of the grain,
> And grapes and healing herbs,
> And fruits and herbage,
> For the service of yourselves and of your cattle.'
>
> (Q. 80: 24-32)

Reflect here over the phrase, 'let man look'. However indifferent man may grow, or avoid to face the realities of life, these realities, will in their extent and universality, always stare him hard in the face. One may shut his eyes to everything in the world ; but he cannot shut them to the means of his own sustenance. Let him look at the food he places before himself. What is it ?—a grain of wheat. Let him place that grain into the hollow of his hand, and let him think over what stages has it not had to pass through before it could emerge in its present form. Was it possible for this insignificant grain to have come into existence had not the entire frame-work of life participated actively in its growth, and that, in a particular manner ? And when such a system of organised coöperation is at work, could it be said that it has no organiser to direct its operation ? In the Chapter *Naḥal*, the argument is presented in another form.

> 'Ye have (also) a lesson in the cattle.
> We give you drink of the pure milk from between dregs and blood, which is in their bellies;—pure beverage palatable to them that quaff it.
> And from the fruits of the palm and the vine, ye get exhilarating drink and healthful nutriment:
> In this, verily, there are signs for those who reflect.
> And thy Lord hath taught the bee, saying:
> Provide thee cells in the mountains, and in the trees, and in the hives which men do build thee.
> Feed then on every kind of fruit, and pursue the ways of your Lord. From its belly cometh forth a fluid of varying hues which yieldeth medicine to man. In this, verily, are signs for the thoughtful.'
>
> (Q. 16:68-71)

Even as the Qur'ān has cited the world of creation as a proof of the existence of a Creator, so also has it referred to the order of life and growth in the Universe not only to prove the existence of a directing mind, but to establish that even as this order is flawless and complete, so is the Mind that regulates it.

One may express this in plainer form. We notice that everything in this world needs sustenance and is provided with it. Surely, there must be some one who could provide it. Who then could it be? Certainly not one who himself is in need of sustenance. Read the following verses where this method of argument is employed:

> 'What think ye? That which ye sow—
> Is it you who cause it to grow, or do we cause it to spring forth?
> If we pleased, we could so make your harvest dry and brittle that ye would lament and say:
> "Truly have we incurred expense, yet are we deprived of harvest."
> What think ye of the water ye drink?
> Is it ye who send it down from the clouds, or we?
> Brackish could we make it, if we pleased?
> Will ye not then be thankful?
> What think ye of the fire you strike?
> Is it ye who rear for it the trees or do we rear?
> It is we who have made it as a remembrancer, and a protection to the way-farer of the desert.'
>
> (Q. 56 : 63-72)

Rububiyat: Proof of the Life Hereafter

The term 'Takhlīq-bil-Ḥaq' further argues the need for 'Life hereafter' or the life after what is called 'death'. That is the goal towards which the life on earth has to move, for, it is unthinkable that man should be created just to live for a few moments and then get annihilated completely. A thing which has been devised with such meticulous care and circumspection has always a meaning to offer and a purpose to serve. An object like the human being, who is made to appear the best of objects on earth and for whose development so much has been carefully provided, is certainly not meant to be a thing which has no better purpose to serve than to strut on earth for a few moments and then disappear for ever. The Creator of the Universe who has created everything for a specific purpose will not throw away the best of his creation, viz., man, as a piece of no value or of little consequence.

> 'What! Do you think that we had created you for pastime and that ye should not be brought back to us?'
>
> (Q. 23: 117)

> 'Have they not considered within themselves that God hath not created the heavens and the earth and all that is between them but for a serious end and for a fixed term? But truly most of them believe not that they shall meet their Lord.'
>
> (Q. 30: 7)

So far, the subject has been presented after the simple manner of the Qur'ān. In the language of science, however, one may state that man is the latest and the noblest link in the process of creative evolution. If we look back, says Mawlana Azad, across time to the very first impulse of life in creation, life on earth will be found to be an immeasurably lengthy process of evolution aiming at, and culminating in the completion of man. In other words, Nature has taken billions and billions of years in its endeavour to give shape to its noblest piece of art, viz. man. Visualize to yourself that far off distant event when this planet of Earth was thrown out of the moulten mass of matter, the Sun, and the long period it must have taken to cool and acquire equable temperature and become fit for life to grow thereon. Who knows how long did it take before the first germ of life, now called protoplasm, could emerge, or how long it took to mould a body for it, and carry it forward from a lower form to a higher, and so on, till it could assume its present human shape. And even then, who knows how long it must have taken to build the requisite intellect for him before man could take his station on the cultural plane. We shall not be wrong if we assert that what all that has been wrought since the formation of the Earth is but one long story of man's growth and development.

'The question arises: Shall an object in the shaping of which Nature has had to make such prolonged careful arrangement was meant just to eat and drink for a little moment on Earth and get extinguished for ever?

A further question arises as a corollary. If the life of man has in the past undergone an endless series of changes only to assume a higher form every time, why should we not expect a continuation of the same process in future? When we are not surprised at the process in the past of one phase of life emerging out of another in succession, why should we grow sceptical, when it is said that the present form of human life disappears only to assume a still higher form?

> 'Thinketh man that he is to be left to drift? Was he not a mere germ in the seminal state, And was he not then made into a clod of blood, Out of which God fashioned him?'
>
> (Q. 75: 36-38)

> 'And surely, from state to state, shall ye be carried forward.'
>
> (Q. 84: 19)

Rububiyat: Proof of Revelation

In like manner the Qur'ān draws from this very order of Rubūbiyat or Divine Providence the principle of good and evil that is to be at work in the life of man and draws also the argument for Divine revelation. It is not conceivable, says Mawlana Azad, that the God of all the Worlds, 'Rabbul ' Ālamīn ', who has provided the means of physical growth and development to everything, should omit to provide for the welfare of the spirit, or that he has not devised a system or law of life which could attend to the spiritual needs of man.

> 'The Revelation of the Book is from God, the Mighty, the Wise !'
>
> (Q. 45: 1)

The Qur'ān is certainly aware of those who doubt the principle of Revelation.

> 'No just estimate do they form of God when they say: Nothing hath God revealed to a human being.'
>
> (Q. 6: 91)

For such, the Qur'ān presents the analogy of the physical world, so as to suggest by implication that even as the physical needs of man are provided in an organized form, so also there does exist a provision for his spiritual needs.

The Rubūbiyat of God is but an aspect of the creative activity of God and springs from the supremely Divine attribute of Rahmat or Graciousness of God, the views on which of Mawlana Azad are set forth in the next chapter.

CHAPTER III

THE ATTRIBUTE OF GRACIOUSNESS

SECTION I : GRACIOUSNESS IN DIVINE SETTING

The system of Rubūbiyat or of Divine providence discussed in the preceding chapter is a striking reality of life. But, points out Mawlana Azad, a greater reality than this is at work everywhere in the Universe and on which this very order of ' Rubūbiyat ' depends ; and it is what the Qur'ān styles as the *Raḥmat* or graciousness or mercy of God which lends beauty or perfection to every object of creation. The divine assurance runs :

> ' My *Raḥmat* encompasses everything in the Universe.'
>
> (Q. 7 : 156)

The principle of *Raḥmat* is pointedly brought to view in the second verse of the opening chapter of the Qur'ān, the *Sūrat-ul-Fātiḥā* and indeed in the formula standing at the head of it,—' In the name of Allah, the Most Gracious, the Most Merciful.' Both the terms used in this verse, *Ar-Raḥmān* and *Ar-Raḥīm*, are derived from *Raḥmat* which denotes the type of tenderness which expresses itself in kindness to others for its own sake and covers in its connotation every aspect of love, affection, benevolence and generosity. *Ar-Raḥmān* means the being who possesses *Raḥmat* and *Ar-Raḥīm* the being who not merely possesses *Raḥmat* but gives perennial expression to it, or a being from whom everything in the Universe derives goodness every moment.

The purpose of the Qur'ān in bringing to mind the two aspects together is to emphasise the all-encompassing character of the *Raḥmat* or the graciousness of God.

The objective of 'Rubūbiyat' is sustenance of life in the Universe. But sustenance alone is not the goal of life. The machinery of life was not worth coming into existence if every action of it were not endowed with the talent to promote steady self-perfection. Philosophy points out that the urge of Nature is to aim at form and beauty. Form demands proportion, and beauty demands harmony. The two constitute the compulsive law of life. But the question arises: Why this compulsiveness? Why harmony alone, and not the reverse of it? Philosophy fails to give an answer to these questionings. In the words of a renowned philosopher 'where "why" begins, philosophy ends'. But the Qur'ān offers an answer. This compulsiveness, it points out, is the compulsiveness of Divine graciousness. The grace of God demands that whatever comes into being must be good and beautiful, and so it is. Asks the Qur'ān:

> 'Say: Whose is all that is in the heavens and the earth?
> Say: God's. He hath imposed graciousness on himself as a Law.'
>
> (Q. 6: 12)

Mawlana Azad draws attention to numerous passages in the Qur'ān which go to emphasize that every object of creation is good in itself and is meant to subserve the welfare of man. This truth is summed up in the following verse:

> 'And He hath subjected to you all that is in the heavens and all that is in the earth. All is

from Him. Verily, herein are signs for those who reflect.'

(Q. 45: 12)

The principle of *Raḥmat*, points out Mawlana Azad, works in such a fashion that all living objects are served simultaneously with what they need without distinction. Even as a man living in a mansion may feel that the entire creation exists only for him, even so, an ant may say that everything is meant to subserve its needs. And who can deny this? Does not the Sun in reality exist to provide warmth to the ant, the rain come to offer moisture to it, and the air waft to bring the smell of sugar to it? Does not the Earth exist to provide the type of shelter that this ant needs in every changing season? The blessings of Nature follow a law of universal and simultaneous application to everything that exists.

> 'No kind of animal is there on Earth, nor bird that flieth with its wings, but they are communities like unto you.'
>
> (Q. 6: 38)

Splitting and Building

One should not forget that the world of life is one of necessary conflict. Here splitting is accompanied by building. Every dispersal has a counter gathering. Even as the breaking of stones is meant only to carve out a thing of beauty, even so, the process of destruction in the Universe only subserves the demands of a beauteous construction. Nature builds every corner of life's edifice assiduously. It moulds every tiny part of it with equal care. In the interest of beauty, it counters obstruction. It is this urge for perfection which sometimes has to produce convulsions or catastrophies, although these are not, in reality, evidence of destruction. In fact, there is no destruction anywhere in life. All that happens is proof of constructiveness. The storms in the oceans, the high floods in the rivers, the volcanic eruptions in mountains, the snow-falls over trees, the hot winds of summer, the thunders of the rainy season, and clouds, and hurricanes—all these may not be pleasing. But the fact is that every disturbing event in the frame-work of life is as much a contributory force to perfection as anything that you may think of. Were there no storms in the ocean, you will not have rain on the plains. Were the clouds to produce no lightning, we shall have no rain at all. Were there no volcanic eruptions in moun-tains, the boiling lava within the bosom of the Earth will burst out and spread over its surface. One may question, why at all there should be boiling lava within the Earth? But we should know that but for it, the quality of growth and development in the things of the earth would never have displayed itself. It is to this truth of life that the Qur'ān draws repeated attention, as for instance—

> 'And of His signs are, that He showeth you the lightning, a source of awe and hope; and that He sendeth down rain from the heaven and giveth life by it to the Earth when dead. Herein are signs for those who understand.'
>
> (Q. 30: 23)

The Beauty of Nature

The greatest blessing of nature, says the Qur'ān, is its beauteous aspect which is but a reflection of the Divine *Raḥmat.* Nature does not simply destroy and construct. It constructs in a manner pleasing to the eye.

In fact, the very nature of the Universe is constituted of beauty. Even as elements are created to give a form to the Universe, even so is it invested with the qualities of colour, light and shade, and of rythm and melody in order to lend beauty to it.

> Such is He who knoweth the invisible and the visible, the Mighty, the Merciful, who hath made everything which He hath created most perfect.
>
> (Q. 32 : 5-6)

There is no doubt that we meet in life things of ugly bearing lying close to objects pleasing to the eye. We listen to the melodious note of the nightingale along with the disturbing cry of the crow. The composite melody of life is to be composed of a diverse variety of notes. Such is the law of harmony in life.

> The seven heavens raise their voice of praise and all who are therein ; neither is there aught which doth not celebrate his praise ; but their notes of praise ye understand not.
>
> (Q. 17 : 47)

Beauty according to the Qur'ān, lies in balance and proportion and these are vouch-safed to every object and there is no flaw in its setting :

> 'Praise the name of thy Lord, the Most High, who hath created and balanced all things.'
>
> (Q. 87 : 1-2)

> 'O man ! Who hath misled thee against thy generous Lord,
> Who hath created thee and moulded thee and shaped thee aright ?'
>
> (Q. 82 : 6-7)

'(Blessed be He) who hath created seven heavens one above another : No defect can'st thou see *in the handiwork of the God of Mercy.* Repeat thy gaze. Seest thou a single flaw ? Then twice more repeat thy gaze : thy gaze will return to thee dulled and weary.'

(Q. 67 : 3-4)

'The handiwork of the God of Mercy' is the term used here. Everything, the Qur'ān points out, is the creation of one who is not merely a creator, but a creator who at the same time is God of Mercy, and that where mercy is at work, there shall dwell beauty and perfection. The display of Raḥmat in life, contends Mawlana Azad, is on that account proof not only of Divine Unity, but of Revelation and the life hereafter.

Zest in Life

Mawlana Azad cites the zest of living noticed in life as a further aspect of Divine Raḥmat or beneficence. The struggle for existence, he points out, is noticeable in every field of life and in every corner of it. Life taken as a whole is a series of trials.

Surely, we have created man to face trials.

(Q. 90 : 4)

Yet, it is so fashioned that under the stress of desires and passions, man enthusiastically engages himself in one or other activity. It is this zest for life that helps him to bear life's difficulties, and extract from it the comfort and happiness that he needs. The greater the difficulties to counter, the greater the zest that one displays for life. Should life be emptied of its trials, man will assuredly feel a void and come to regard it as not worth pursuing. The observation is endorsed by Mawlana

Azad by a reference to a variety of human experiences and even to the variegated behaviour of Nature. He particularly draws attention to the law of *Tazwīj* or of producing a thing by two's, as a contributory force to zest in living. Nothing is produced solitarily single, says he. It always comes out in two's, one being a complement to the other. The day has its counter part in the night; the morning in the evening; the male in the female species, and life in death.

> And of everything, have we created pairs; that haply ye may reflect.
>
> (Q. 51:49)

> Glory be to Him, who hath created pairs of all things, of what the Earth groweth, and of mankind themselves, and of things beyond their ken.
>
> (Q. 36:36)

It is this law of Nature which infuses into man and woman the talent for mutual attraction, providing thereby the requisite opportunity for family life.

> Creator of the heavens and of the earth! He hath given you mates from among your own selves, and cattle, male and female—by this means to multiply you.
>
> (Q. 42:9)

The Qur'ān states that this arrangement is devised to induce love between them and peace of mind, so that through their joint co-operation, they might with confidence bear and counter the trials of life.

> And one of his signs it is, that he hath created mates for you of your own species, that ye may

> dwell with them, and hath put love and tenderness between you. Herein truly are signs for those who reflect.
>
> (Q. 30 : 20)

Survival of the useful

A form of life meant to display beauty, says Mawlana Azad, would not have maintained itself for long unless provision was made to sustain that beauty and rid it of all that affected it. Nature is ever at work to clear the weeds and preserve that which deserves preservation. This process is loosely styled as the 'survival of the fittest'. But the Quranic emphasis is not on the physical aspect of things but on one's usefulness to life in general. It points out that only that continues to live which has some usefulness about it, or something good to offer to life.

> 'He sendeth down the rain from heaven; then flow the torrents in their due measure, and the flood beareth along swelling foam. And from the metals which are molten in the fire for the sake of ornaments or utensils, a like foam ariseth. As to the foam, it is quietly gone: and as to what is useful to man, it remaineth on the earth.'
>
> (Q. 13 : 17)

The Decree of Truth

The Qur'ān argues that just as in the physical aspect of the world that which is most useful to life survives, even so, in the inward aspect, only that which is most useful to it should survive? In this connection, the Qur'ān uses two terms—*Ḥaq* and *Bāṭil*, truth and falsehood.

In Arabic, the root word *Ḥaqaq* signifies stability or durability. That which is lasting is *Ḥaq*. *Bāṭil* is just the opposite of it, or that which is not lasting. So, whenever there is a conflict between *Ḥaq* and *Bāṭil*, the success rests with Ḥaq. That is what the Qur'ān calls *Qaḍā bil Ḥaq*, the decree of truth.

> And say : Truth is come, and falsehood is vanished.
> Verily, falsehood is a thing that vanisheth.
>
> (Q. 17:83)

Whenever the term Ḥaq is used, the Qur'ān not only advances the claim of truth to durability, to its right to prevail, but sets the criterion by which one might easily distinguish between what is Ḥaq and what is Bāṭil, what is to endure and what is to disappear ; so much so, that the attributive term is applied not only to God, the Ever True, the Everlasting, *Al-Ḥaq*, but to the revealed word of God or Revelation as well.

Were it not for Nature's excision of what is not useful to life and the preservation of what is useful to it, there would have been chaos in life.

> But if truth had followed in the train of their desires, the heavens and the earth and all that therein is, had surely come to ruin.
>
> (Q. 23 : 73)

But the law of truth does not assert that every 'Bāṭil' or untruth or that which is not useful to life must necessarily be extinguished forthwith or that every expression of truth should produce an immediate effect. Such a line of action is repugnant to the law of *Raḥmat*. Even as in the outward physical world, so also in the inward life of man, the law of steady movement prevails. It allows time for reflection and for making amends. Else, no one or no group of people indulging in wickedness will survive for a moment.

> ' Should God hastên (the consequence of) evil on men as they fain would hasten their good, then were their end decreed.'
>
> (Q. 10 : 12)

Process : Gradual

The laws of nature are so devised that they do not work for sudden or dramatic metamorphosis in anything. On the other hand, they proceed on certain steady lines. Their movement or operation follows a gradual process. The Qur'ān makes this clear. While it affirms ' that whatever (law of life) we have decreed, is unalterable ', it points out at the same time that ' we do not impose any undue hardship on man on that account'. (Q. 50: 28). Nature has fixed for everything a period of rise, and a period of decline, slow and steady either way. The phenomenon is observable not merely in the life of man, but in the life of every other object of creation. For everything is set a period, or *'ajl* as styled by the Qur'ān, and it varies with every object of creation.

This process of steady movement is evidently intended, in its application to human life, to help man pause and reflect at every stage and adjust himself with the laws operating in the process. The provision of this opportunity for correction is a provision of *Raḥmat* or the grace of God. The Qur'ān says that were this provision absent from life's equipment, none would have profited by life, and every slip would have spelt ruination to it.

> ' If God should chastise men according to their deserts, he would not leave any moving thing on the surface of the earth. But for an appointed

term, doth He respite them. And when their time shall come, then verily God's eye is on His servants.'

(Q. 35: 45)

The process applies equally well to the upward and the downward march in life. In the upward march, it allows time for easy gathering of perfection from stage to stage ; and on the downward path, it allows time for correction.

> To all—both to these and those, the good and the bad people, do we prolong the gifts of thy Lord ; for not to any shall the gifts of thy Lord be denied.
>
> (Q. 17: 21)

Purposive latitude

If man desires to profit by the latitude furnished by this process, he can in proper time make amends for every mishap, and march upward. On the other hand, if he misses the opportunities so afforded, he steadily goes down till the inevitable decree, implicit in his behaviour, overtakes him.

> And when their time is come they shall not delay or advance it an hour.
>
> (Q. 16: 61)

The Qur'ān points out that every action in life takes its own time to produce its result. For everything a measure of time is measured out.

> ' But if they turn their backs, say : I have warned you all alike ; but I know not whether that with which ye are threatened be nigh or distant.'
>
> (Q. 21 : 109)

But the Qur'ān asks us not to apply our sense of time to everything in life. The operation of nature is such that even the greatest computation of time according to our time-sense may be but a day for it.

> And they will bid thee to hasten the chastisement. But God cannot fail His warning. And verily, a day with thy Lord is as a thousand years, as ye reckon them !
>
> How many cities have I long borne with, wicked though they were, yet then laid hold on them to chastise them ! Unto Me shall all return.
>
> (Q. 22 : 46, 47)

People generally expect immediate results for what they do. The Arabs of the Prophet's time, who dissented from him, used to taunt him with the observation that were their ways really evil, they should meet with instantaneous punishment. But they forget that the delay in the emergence of effect is only meant to give time for them to repent and make amends. Such is the law of *Raḥmat* at work in life.

> And they say : When will this [illegible]se be made good, if ye speak true ? '
>
> Say : Haply a part of what ye desire to be hastened may be close behind you.
>
> And truly, the Lord is full of goodness towards men : but most of them are not thankful.
>
> (Q. 27 : 73-75)

> They will challenge thee to hasten the punishment : but had there not been a season fixed for it, that punishment had already come upon

> them. But it shall overtake them when they look not for it.
>
> (Q. 29: 53)
>
> Nor do we delay it, but until a time appointed.
>
> (Q. 11: 106)

The point to note is not what time an evil action takes to produce its result, but what type of people really triumph in the end. The Qur'ān asserts that it is the righteous who will succeed in the end.

> Say: O my people! Act as ye may choose to act; I indeed will act my part, and ye shall know whose is the final goal? Undoubtedly the unjust will not prosper.
>
> (Q. 6: 135)

The Qur'ān enunciates the principle that wickedness in all forms is bound to fail and that goodness is bound to succeed. Wherever this principle is referred to or emphasised in the Qur'ān, it is expressed in terms such as, 'Surely those who transgress shall not prosper,' (6:21)—'Surely, the wicked shall not prosper', (10: 18) —'God prospereth not the work of the evil-doers,' (10: 81)—'God guideth not the people who do not believe', (9: 37)—'God guideth not the people who transgress', (3: 80) and so forth.

The principle underlying here does not suggest that the door of guidance or correction is wilfully closed or that those falling under these categories will be misled. It is a matter of regret that the commentators of the Qur'ān have failed to understand the significance of the technique observed by the Qur'ān. What the Qur'ān states is that notwithstanding the fact that the law of causation is at work in life, the *Raḥmat* of God offers to man opportunities of correction, and that when these are disregarded or, in other words, when guidance is flouted, that the law takes its inevitable course. The term employed by the Qur'ān for opportunities of improvement is *Tamattu'* and is applicable to all conditions of life and is afforded to every one without distinction. Says the Qur'ān :

> 'Yes ! We have given these men and their fathers opportunities for profiting even by lengthened lives.'
>
> (Q. 21 : 45)

Expressions occurring in the Qur'ān like, 'We gave them respite for a while—that they may enjoy themselves awhile', 'Enjoy yourselves then ; but in the end, ye shall know (the truth)', and so on, go only to emphasise the principle under consideration.

'The Decree of Truth, and Nations.'

The law of 'Truth' or of survival is applicable to groups of people or nations even as to individuals, and determines the conditions of their rise and fall. The Qur'ān points out that even as in the case of individuals, so in the case of nations, every group of people which has no use or value to life is eliminated. Only they live or survive who subserve or advance the cause of life. That is the Law of *Raḥmat.* For otherwise, human wickedness will have no check placed thereon.

> 'And were it not for the restraint of one by means of others imposed on men by God, verily, the earth had been utterly corrupted. But God is bounteous to his creatures.'
>
> (Q. 2 : 252)

The same truth is expressed in the following words:

> 'And if God had not repelled some men by others, cloisters, and churches, and synagogues, and mosques wherein the name of God is ever commemorated, would surely have been destroyed.'
>
> (Q. 22 : 41)

Process gradual

Even as in the life of things, a process of gradual effect is at work in the life also of nations. The door for returning to the good-way or for self-correction is always open to them; for, such is the principle of *Raḥmat* governing all life.

> 'And we have distributed them in the earth as (separate) peoples. Some of them are upright and some are otherwise; and by good things and by unpleasant things do we test them in order that they might return to us.'
>
> (Q. 7 : 167)

Even for nations as for individuals, a time limit is set during which they will have to return to the straight path, if, on any account, they have strayed away from it.

> 'Do they not see that they are put on trial every year once or twice? Yet they neither repent nor do they heed the warning.'
>
> (Q. 9 : 127)

If opportunities thus afforded are missed, the law takes its course.

> 'Every nation hath its set time. And when their time is come, they shall not retard it an hour, and they shall not advance it.'
>
> (Q. 7 : 32)

> 'We have never destroyed a city except that whose term (according to the law of life) was fixed.
> No people can foretell or retard its destiny.'
>
> (Q. 15 : 4-5)

The same law weeds out the undesirables,—those not useful to human life—and instals others in their place to carry out the purposes of life.

> This, because thy Lord will not destroy the cities in their sin, while their people are yet unconscious of the wrong they do.
> And for all, are grades of recompense as the result of their deeds ; and of what they do, thy Lord is not regardless.
> And thy Lord is self-sufficient, the Lord of Mercy. If he please, he may remove you and cause whom He will to take your place, even as he had caused you to succeed those who had sprung from a different seed.
>
> (Q. 6 : 131 - 133)

In the latitude and the opportunities for self-correction given to man, Mawlana Azad reads the most striking expression of divine *Raḥmat.* It is true that the Qur'ān emphasises that every action has its inevitable reaction or result. But at the same time, it makes it clear that this law does not close its door for correction. In fact, opportunities for making amends are provided to every one at every turn. They are always close at hand. The moment one begins to feel repentent, the force of mercy is promptly released, and every drop of tear one sheds in contrition washes a stain of sin and one feels that he had never committed any sin at all. As the Prophet has said : 'One who repents sincerely is like one who has never committed any sin.' Says the Qur'ān:

> 'Those who shall repent and believe and do good deed—for them God will change their evil deeds into good deeds, for, God is Gracious, Merciful.'
>
> (Q. 25 : 70)

The scope of Divine forgiveness, as depicted by the Qur'ān, is vast, and unlimited. However serious the sin committed, whatever the nature of one's wickedness and whatever the period in which one has lived in sin, the moment one feels repentent and sincerely knocks at the door of mercy, the response is forgiveness.

> 'O My servants, who have transgressed to your own hurt, despair not of God's Mercy, for all sins doth God forgive. Gracious, Merciful is He.'
>
> (Q. 39 : 54)

SECTION II

GRACIOUSNESS IN HUMAN SETTING

The question at this stage arises : what is the Quranic objective in drawing attention to divine attributes, particularly the attribute of *Raḥmat* which, as Mawlana Azad points out, permeates every other attribute and imparts to each its qualifying touch ? The answer is given by the Prophet in his noble injunction: 'Develop in yourself the attributes of God.' And since *Raḥmat* is an all-embracing divine attribute, it follows that the primary objective of man should be to give to every thought and activity, whatever the field—social, economic or political—the touch of this great quality.

Bond of love between God and Man—The Qur'ān makes it clear that the bond subsisting between God and His creation, mankind, is one of love.

> Yet there are men who take to them images along with God, and love them with the love that should truly be shown to God. But in the faithful, the love of God is the stronger !
>
> (Q. 2 : 161)

> Say : If ye love God, follow me : God will love you, and forgive your sins, for God is Forgiving Merciful.
>
> (Q. 3 : 29)

Over and over again the Qur'ān emphasises that belief in God must necessarily result in the love of God.

> O ye who believe ! should any of you desert this path, God will then raise up a people loved by Him, and loving Him.
>
> (Q. 5 : 59)

The Qur'ān points out that the love of God is to be expressed through one's love of God's creatures. He who desires to love God has necessarily to learn to love his creatures.

> 'Who for love of God disburseth his wealth etc.'
>
> (Q. 2 : 172)

> Who though longing for it themselves, bestow their food on the poor and the orphan and the captive, (and say) :

> 'We feed you for the sake of God: We seek from you neither recompense nor thanks.'
>
> (Q. 76:8-9)

This truth has been expressed impressively in a tradition of the Prophet. 'On the day of Judgment, God will address a particular individual: "O son of Adam! I was sick, but you did not attend on me." Bewildered, this individual will say: "How is that possible? You are after all the Supreme Lord of all the Worlds, (and cannot fall sick)." God will reply: "Do not you remember that so and so among my servants was ill and lying close to you, and you did not turn to him in sympathy. If you had but gone near him, you would have found me beside him." In like manner, God will address another individual: "O son of Adam! I had asked of you a piece of bread; but you would not give it to me." The individual will submit: "How is that possible? Could God need bread?" And God will reply: "Do not you remember that so and so among my servants had in a moment of hunger asked of you bread, and did you not refuse to give it to him? If you had given him food, you would have found me beside him." Similarly, God will ask yet another individual: "O son of Adam! I had asked of you a cup of water, but you did not give it to me." The individual will cry out: "How is that possible? How can God feel thirsty?" God will reply: "So and so of my servants who was thirsty asked of you water, but you did not give it to him. If you had given it to him, you would surely have found me beside him."

Deeds and prayer

The same consideration is implicit in the various forms of devotion and action suggested for man by the Qur'ān. It is implicit also in the emphasis it lays on specific virtues or qualities one has to develop and is implicit also in the distinction made between what is lawful and what is not lawful. So great is the stress laid on the presence in man of the quality of Raḥmat or mercy ! Indeed, on no other attribute of God does it lay the stress that it lays on this attribute. The references to it occur in more than 300 places of the Qur'ān; and if we include other attributes which in one form or another are concomitants of it, such as providence, benevolence, forbearance, and forgiveness, the number enlarges, so much so, that the Qur'ān from cover to cover assumes the role of but a single unified message of divine mercy. Indeed, the life and teaching of the Prophet of Islam may be expressed in a phrase—worship of One God and love of His creation. A well-known Ḥadith states that the mercy of God is for those who show mercy to God's creatures. Christ's famous saying runs : ' Show kindness to those who live on earth, so that he who is in Heaven may show kindness to you '. In precisely the same style the Prophet of Islam said, ' Graciously kind is God, the Holy the High. Show kindness to those on earth so that Divine grace may descend upon you from above.' Many a Ḥadith may be quoted wherein it is said that God's mercy is for those who show mercy to others, though the object of mercy may be as insignificant a thing as a sparrow.

The fact is that the basis of devotion to God, according to the Qur'ān, rests on the idea that the aim of human life is to reflect in one's own thought and activity the attributes of God. The Qur'ān regards the emergence of man as the line where animality ceases to exist and a higher life begins. The quality which distinguishes man from the mere animal and which gives him his pre-eminent station in the scale of life is his humanity, which the Qur'ān styles as the spirit of God.

> 'Then shaped him and breathed of His spirit into Him, and gave you hearing and seeing and heart.'
>
> (Q. 32 : 9)

The above verse makes it explicit that man's position in the scale of life is so high that God himself has breathed His spirit into him, or in other words, that man *is endowed* with the requisite talent to exercise *Rahmat* or mercy in relation to his external world.

So, wherever the Qur'ān attempts to raise before our mind the concept of Divine mercy, it does so with the purpose of stimulating in us the quality of mercy. The same is the purpose underlying references to all other attributes. The quality on which it lays its supreme emphasis is the quality of forgiveness. This is the perennial theme of the Qur'ān. Of course, the Qur'ān does not call on man to love his enemy ; but it calls on him to exercise forgiveness, for, he who learns to forgive his enemies deserves forgiveness from God. That is the way to purification.

> 'Who master their anger, and forgive others ! God loveth the doers of good.'
>
> (Q. 3 : 1?3)

> 'Moreover, good and evil are not to be treated alike. Turn away evil by what is better, and lo ! he between whom and thyself was enmity, shall be as though he were a warm friend. But none attain to this save men steadfast in patience and none attain to it except the most highly favoured.'
>
> (Q. 41 : 34-35)

The Qur'ān does not discourage retaliation altogether. But wherever it has permitted it, it has done so in the interest of security of life. But it may be noted that wherever such permission is given, there is always the rider going with it, that forgiveness is a better procedure and that it is graceful to do good to those who wrong you.

> If you at all retaliate, then retaliate to the same extent that ye were injured; but if ye can endure patiently, best will it be for those who patiently endure.
>
> Endure then with patience. But thy patient endurance must be sought in none but God.
>
> (Q. 16:126-127)

> And who so beareth wrongs with patience and forgiveth—this verily is high-mindedness.
>
> (Q. 42:40)

The Evangel and the Qur'an

We have just pointed out that the Qur'ān does not state that you should love your enemies. The statement requires a little elucidation.

Christ had to counter the religious hypocracy of the Jews and their lack of morality by his message of love and forgiveness and purity of life. Hence it was that in the New Testament we meet expressions such as these :

> 'Ye have heard that it hath been said, An eye for an eye, and a tooth for a tooth : But I say unto you : That ye resist not evil : but Whosoever shall smite thee on the right cheek, turn to him the other also.
>
> You have heard that it hath been said thou shalt love thy neighbour, and hate thine enemy. But

> I say unto you, love your enemies, bless them that curse you, do good to them that hate you, and pray for them which despitefully use you, and persecute you.' (S. Matthew 5:38-39, 43-44)

But what was the significance of these expressions? Was it a call for spiritual purification, or was it a laying down of a code of law?

Neglect of Christ's Message: It is a matter for regret, observes Mawlana Azad, that the followers of the Bible and its critics have both, in their several ways, misunderstood these statements of Christ. Both have treated them as definite rules of conduct to be scrupulously observed, and both have had in consequence to admit that they are impracticable. The Christians while admitting their impracticability, console themselves with the thought that saints and martyrs among them, at any rate, did act up to these rules of conduct. Their detractors, on the other hand, have persisted in stressing that these rules of conduct run counter to human nature and are of no practical value to life. Clearly history has done a great wrong to this great teacher of mankind. The unsympathetic critic has made no effort to understand Christ's message, and the ignorant believer in him has avoided to catch its real significance. Was the message of Christ really impracticable? Was it repugnant to human nature? To admit the questions is to knock the bottom out of the very Quranic assertion that the message of all the Prophets has been one and the same.

Reality about Christ's Message: The trouble with the message of Christ lies in the failure of his followers to understand its true purpose. Christ appeared during a period of history when the Jewish morality had reached its lowest ebb, and when purity of life had given way to outward ritual passing for devotion to God. The condition of the neighbouring nations—the Romans, the Egyptians, and the Assyrians—was more or less the same. These people failed to appreciate that Christ's message of love and forgiveness was really meant to arrest the prevailing tendency towards evil life. To enjoy the killing of helpless people, to subject individuals accused of crime to a variety of novel ways of torture, to throw human beings to ferocious animals, and to burn down wilfilly populous towns, to regard and treat all aliens as slaves, and to exult in cruelty were features of the Roman culture, and pastimes of the Egyptian and Assyrian demi-gods. The cry of the hour was the emergence of a warner and a messenger of love laying stress on the purity of heart. And this warner and messenger appeared in the person of Christ, who stressed the importance of the inner life as against the outward, and tried to revive for man the forgotten but eternal message of humanity and love.

The inspired utterance of Christ has a natural figurative charm about it. Those who can conjure up the vision of a Trinity and Redemption and Atonement are hardly the type of people who can comprehend fully the significance of the figurative touches that Christ gave to his utterance. By interpreting everything too literally, they have missed him.

Wherever Christ has said ' Love your enemies ', his meaning was certainly not that one should grow into a devoted lover of his enemies. On the other hand, his plain meaning was that instead of exciting in oneself the feeling of anger, hatred or revenge, one should develop the feeling of pity and forgiveness. In a society where one hated one's own kith and kin, the appeal : ' love your enemy ' was indeed an appeal for giving up hatred. That is the style of Christ. Take another of his well-known expression: 'Turn the other cheek also.' Surely, Christ never meant that you should literally do so. His clear meaning was that one should develop the feeling of forgiveness or forbearance. To take the literal sense of every figurative expression is not the way of the cultured mind. Should we do so, the entire corpus of inspired or revealed literature will straightaway present the spectacle of an incoherent jumble.

There is no doubt that religion and law have prescribed punishment for wrong-doing. For the safety of society this is necessary. But the thought of 'punishment' is entertained or tolerated for the simple reason that a lesser evil should operate as a preventive of a greater evil. That is the object of punishment from a purely religious standpoint. It is a measure of correction. But man has employed this institution of correction for the destruction of human life. In fact, more desolation and ruin has been wrought by the exponents of law and religion than by any other. If we should ask history to show who has wrought greater havoc to humanity outside the sphere of war, it will surely point its finger at the engines of destruction, the religious tribunals, and the inquisitions which have been set up by the dispensers of religion and law. The purpose of Christ was to inculcate in man the feeling of love, and certainly not to lay down a law against the punishment of crime. His aim was to let man rest his action on love, and take to punishment or retaliation only in the last resort and only as a corrective.

The followers of the law of Moses had rendered the law into an instrument of punishment only. Christ tried to bring home to them that the law was not meant to deal punishment, but to point the way to salvation, and that the way to salvation was the way of love and mercy.

Actor and Action—The initial mistake which man has made is his failure to distinguish between action and actor. Religion makes a clear distinction. The aim of all religions has been to inculcate in man the sense of dislike for sin, and not for man, the doer of sin. They have certainly enjoined that we should hate sin; they have certainly not asked us to hate the sinner. They merely resemble a physician who may draw a dark picture of an ailment, but who nevertheless tenderly takes care of the patient. The physician's tenderness and care increase with the increase in the ailment with which he is afflicted. Such also is the function of the healers of spiritual diseases. They do not hate the sinner. They pity him, on the other hand, and are full of benevolence towards him. They certainly do want us to hate sin, but they do not ask us to hate the sinner. It is this distinction which our religious divines have failed to grasp in the course of history. The message of Christ was that we should hate sin, but should take care of the sinner and treat him with compassion and love, in order that he might rectify his past and be a gain to human life. That is why some of the early followers of the Prophet have said: 'the humility of sinners is liked by God better than the dignified ritualistic postures of the pious'.

It may be noted here that wherever God addresses sinners in the Qur'ān or refers to them, the usual form is that of the personal possessive which denotes tenderness.

> 'O *my* servants who have transgressed to your own hurt!'
>
> (Q. 39:53)

> 'Was it ye who led these *my* servants astray!'
>
> (Q. 25:17)

This form of address bears resemblance to the form which a father usually adopts when speaking to his son: 'O my son! In commenting upon the above verse from the 'Surat-ul-Zumar', Imam Ja'far as-Ṣādiq, the great-grandson of the Prophet, observed: 'Whenever we call our children, they run to us without entertaining the slightest fear; for, they feel certain that the parent could never be cruel to them. More than twenty times is the phrase "O my servants" or "O my people" used in the Qur'ān. This style of address is employed even in the case of the worst sinners. Could there be a better proof than this of the essential mercy of God shown in his dealings with His creatures'?

No conflict between the teachings of the Qur'ān and the Bible.

There is thus really no difference, says Mawlana Azad, between the teachings of the Qur'ān and the teachings of Christ. The injunctions of both are the same. Only, the style employed in expression and the occasion for the utterance vary. Christ stressed the need for purification of the heart, and did not attempt to lay down a law, for the law of Moses was there, and he did not choose to alter it. He merely desired that this law should be applied to purify the spirit. The Qur'ān, however, presents ethics and law simultaneously. Naturally therefore it has had to assume a style and expression which should create no doubts as to the purposes to be served. In the first place, it calls upon man to develop the talent for forgiveness, as it regards it the basis on which all piety and righteousness should rest. In the second, it keeps open the door for retaliation in unavoidable contingencies. In the third, it is careful to make it clear that retaliation should not err on the side of excess, as that would be decided injustice. This attitude is common to all religions.

> 'And who, when a wrong is done them, redress themselves—yet let the recompense of evil be only a like evil—but he who forgiveth and worketh reform in the wrong-doer, shall be rewarded by God Himself; for He loveth not those who act unjustly.
>
> And there shall be no way open against those who, after being wronged, retaliate; But there shall be a way open against those who unjustly wrong others, and act insolently on the Earth in disregard of justice. A grievous punishment doth await them.
>
> And whoso beareth wrong with patience and forgiveth; this verily is high-mindedness.'
>
> (Q. 42:39-43)

The emphasis here is on forgiveness. The door for retaliation is necessarily kept open; but the way to righteousness lies primarily through forgiveness. The Qur'ān does not regard retaliation as a virtue. It calls it " a like evil " and surely an evil can never be a virtue. But the door is kept open for it lest a greater evil follow. The forgiver is here regarded as one who sets right or effects improvement. It, therefore, follows that only those really contribute to perfection in life who exercise forgiveness.

The question may be asked: If the essential teaching of the Qur'ān is one of mercy or *Raḥmat*, how is it that the Qur'ān is harsh on those who do not accept its message? A detailed answer to this question will be furnished in a more appropriate place later on. But here a passing explanation may be offered. There is no doubt that the Qur'ān expresses itself in very strong terms here and there against those who had refused to accept its message in the time of the Prophet. But the question is who were exactly those whom the Qur'ān had in view? Does the Qur'ān express itself strongly against those who differed in view, or against those who resorted to violence against its message. Even a cursory glance of the Qur'ān will make it clear that the remonstrance of the Qur'ān is for those who had wilfully persecuted the followers of the Qur'ān, and displayed violent hostility towards them. To show mercy to such would be a disservice to the cause of humanity. It would be a mercy subserving the interests of wickedness or of cruelty and injustice.

Be it noted that the Qur'ān speaks of the Divine attribute of mercy in conjunction with the attribute of justice which is discussed in the following chapter. It does not isolate justice from mercy, but regards justice as mercy itself. It states that one cannot display in his life the sense of humanity unless at the same time one sets one's face against every form of cruelty. In the New Testament, we find that Christ was obliged to style the disturbers of life in his time as 'a brood of serpents and a gang of dacoits'.

Kufr : simple and violent—The Qur'ān uses the term 'kufr' in the sense of 'denial' and this is of two kinds, 'simple' and 'violent'. Simple Kufr or denial may take several forms. A person may not agree with your teaching, may not understand it or appreciate it, either because he has no urge to know a new thing, or he is content with his own way of life. This is simple denial. To such, the Qur'ān asks the Prophet to say 'To you your way, and to me mine'. On the other hand, the 'violent denial' differs from the simple denial in this that one wilfully sets his face against you, and tries by every possible method to harm and ruin you, and allows you no rest to speak out the truth that you have. It is about such people that the Qur'ān remarks in a style which may appear strong.

> 'Hearts have they with which they understand not, and eyes have they with which they see not, and ears have they with which they hear not. They are like brutes : yea, they go more astray : these are the heedless.'
>
> (Q. 7 : 179)

Whenever there has been a call going forth in the history of man, some have accepted it, some have refused to accept and some have deliberately and violently opposed it. The Qur'ān had to deal with all the three categories of people. The first category, it received into its fold and gave them the training they needed. To the second, it conveyed its message and left them to reflect over it. 'There is no compulsion in religion,' it announced. With the third, it remonstrated in strong terms ; for, to have done otherwise, would have been an abject yielding to violence in thought and deed, and would have been against the law of nature. Raḥmat (Mercy) always goes with justice. The law is at work in the phenomenal world and must necessarily be observed in relation to the inward world of man as well.

CHAPTER IV

THE ATTRIBUTE OF JUSTICE

The attribute of God which the Qur'ān refers to in continuation of its reference to the attributes of Providence and Mercy is that of justice.

According to the Qur'ān, points out Mawlana Azad, Divine Justice is not something arbitrarily imposed, as was the idea prevailing when the Qur'ān was delivered, but that, on the other hand, it is the inevitable result of one's own action, or 'what one earns for himself.' The old belief had been inspired by the absolutism or despotism of rulers, and a similitude entertained in respect of God, suggesting that, even as absolute monarchs, God dispensed reward or punishment as His whim suggested. This was why people in those days propitiated God by various forms of sacrifice. The idea was to humour him up and keep his temper equable or at the normal.

Among the Jews and the Christians, the concept of God had, no doubt, been raised a little higher; but the essential character of the earlier common belief still clung to them. The Jews believed that God was even like the deities of others an absolute dictator. If he was pleased with them, He would style Himself as the God of Israel. If displeased, He would wreak His vengeance and cause their ruination. The Christian view was no better. Because of their belief in the original sin of Adam, the entire race of Adam or mankind had become an object of Divine displeasure and that consequently Christ had to atone for this original sin through his own crucification and effect the redemption of man.

But the Qur'ān places the concept of reward or

punishment on a different footing. It does not regard the treatment meted out to man, whether reward or punishment, as something different from the law of life at work in the Universe. The Qur'ān asserts that a universal law of causation is in operation in every sphere of life. Everything has a quality of its own—thought, feeling, or action—and produces a result germane or appropriate to it. That is its requital, its recompense, its reward or punishment. The result of a good action is good and that is one's reward. Similarly, the result of an evil action is evil, and that is his punishment. The one is designated Heaven, and the other Hell.

The Qur'ān points out that everything in the phenomenal world is invested with a nature peculiar to it. So is it also with every type of human action. Every action produces a result peculiar to it. That is what the Qur'ān calls recompense, requital, or justice.

> 'Deem they whose earnings are only evil, that we will deal with them as with those who believe and work righteousness, so that their lives and deaths shall be alike ? I'll do they judge.
>
> In all truth hath God created the heavens and the earth, that he may reward every one as he shall have wrought, and they shall not be wronged.'
>
> (Q. 45: 21-22)

For this reason, the Qur'ān calls every action, good or bad, as 'Kasab'. 'Kasab' in Arabic literally means what one earns or the result of one's action. 'Kasab' acquired, and shall bear the evil to acquire which it hath laboured.'

(Q. 2: 286)

'He who doth right—it is for himself: and he who doth evil—it is for himself; and thy Lord will not deal unfairly with his servants.'

(Q. 41: 46)

The same principle applies to the actions of communities or nations.

'Those people have now passed away: They have the reward of their deeds, and for you is the meed of yours.'

(Q. 2: 134)

A well-known Ḥadith of the Prophet draws attention to this principle of life:

'God says: "O my people! if all those who are already born or will be born hereafter, and if all human beings and all jinns should be as good as the most righteous among you, it will not add a whit to My sovereignty over the world. O my people! in like manner, if all those who have gone before, and those who will come after, and all human beings and jinns should be as wicked as the most wicked among you, it will not detract a whit from My sovereignty. O my people! if all those who have gone before and all those who may come after you should assemble at a place and each one of them should ask of Me a gift and I grant the prayer of each, it will not diminish My store-house of mercy and benevolence even to the extent of a single drop taken out of an ocean. O my people! remember, that it is your own deeds over which, for your sake, I keep watch and return to you. So, whosoever gets a pleasing requital for his action, let him offer his thanks to God; and whosoever receives an unpleasant requital for his action, let him blame himself for it, and none else".'

(Muslim : Abu-Dhar).

Let it not be supposed that reward or punishment depends upon God's pleasure or displeasure. What the Qur'ān states is this that all recompense or reward or punishment is directly the result of one's own action and that God is pleased with a good action and displeased with an evil one. This concept is at variance or in conflict with earlier beliefs. 'Ad-Dīn' is an apt term to denote the law at work in life, and should set at rest all misconceptions prevailing on the subject. Its use in the 'Surat-ul-Fātiḥa' brings out in clear perspective the significance of the good or the evil which flows from an action, regarded either as reward or punishment.

Further, it should be noted that the Qur'ān having drawn attention to God's attributes of 'Rubūbiyat' and 'Raḥmat' (Mercy or Grace), does not straightaway proceed to speak of the opposite attributes of terror and majesty. On the other hand, it speaks of God as the Master of the Day of Requital', thereby drawing atten-tion to the attribute implicit in the twin attributes of 'Rubūbiyat' and 'Raḥmat', viz. the attribute of 'Justice'. Sheer terror for its own sake has no place in the scheme of divine attributes. It is all justice, productive, in one of its aspects, of 'awe' or 'fear' operating only for the good of man.

This aspect of Divine activity, the mind of man could not catch easily, and has often blundered in consequence. It assigned all unpleasant happenings of life to divine displeasure, by conjuring up attributes of terror and pressure for God, although had it striven to probe the reality, it would have realized that what is ascribed as divine displeasure was in fact an aspect of Divine mercy itself. If the law of requital were not in operation in the life of the Universe, or were not the process of perfection to demand the elimination of all that clogs the path of perfection, there would have been no sense of balance or justice operating for good in life, and the result would have been chaos.

Even as the world of creation depends for its existence on the *Rubūbiyat* and *Raḥmat* of God, even so, does it depend for its perfection on His attribute of dispensing justice to everything. Providence and Mercy provide all that life needs, and the principle of justice gives it the balance or beauty that it needs by eliminating every ugliness lurking therein. For, if one should look deeply into this aspect of life, it will be realized that it is the force of justice that is responsible for whatever order or beauty that there is in life.

Justice or ' 'Adl ' in Arabic means ' to make even '. A court of Justice is intended to soften down angularities of contending parties appearing before it "Adl" or justice is used also in the sense of ' scales ' whereby the two sides are made to show equal weight. Justice introduces balance in life, and makes one thing agree with another, and produce unity or harmony. It is this principle which is responsible for beauty and proportion in every form of thought and life. It is really the basis on which the scheme of the Universe rests. Every planet and every star is functioning in space in balanced or just or right relation with one another. It is this very principle which keeps together a society. Even a little slackening of this principle in the physical world of matter will result in disorder.

The Qur'ān asks us to consider whether this principle of justice which is so clearly at work in the phenomenal world of matter, will leave out human activity from its sphere of operation. It is why the Qur'ān calls all balanced action, whatever the field of life, as ''Amal-e-Ṣāleh' or righteous action. Further, whatever terms the Qur'ān has used for all forms of unrighteous or evil activities are all intended to convey the thought that they contravene this principle of justice, terms such as *ẓulm*, *Ṭughyān*, *Isrāf*, *Tabdhīr*, *Ifsād*, *I'tidā*, and '*Udwān*. What we call 'ẓulm' in Arabic has been defined as that which is not 'in proper form' or 'not in order'. It is why the term 'shirk' or 'associating anything with God, is described as the greatest of 'ẓulm', for nothing more 'improper' is possible to conceive of. It is obvious that anything which is out of place or not in order is the negation of balance or justice. Similarly, the term 'Ṭughyān' means 'excess' or 'over and above the proper measure'. When the river is in floods or overflows its banks or its flow is in excess of the normal, the term 'Ṭughyān' is used. Such a state is opposed to normality or balance or justice. Similarly, the term 'Isrāf' (wastage), 'Tabdhīr' (mis-use) and 'Ifsād' (disorder, mischief) fall under this category, as also I'tidā' and ''Udwān', which both mean 'going beyond one's bounds'. Everything therefore which is out of place is a clog in the way of perfection and has to be countered; and this is done by the application of justice which, according to the Qur'ān, is an expression of the 'Raḥmat' or Mercy or Grace of God.

CHAPTER V

UNITY OF REVELATION

The Law of Requital which was the subject of consideration in the previous chapter deals with the question of human responsibilities. Every action has its reaction. The good or the evil which befalls a man is the result of his own action. That being so, the question arises : Does the *Rubūbiyat* of God which aims to offer provision for development afford man the talent to face with confidence the responsibilities with which he is charged in life ? In other words, has he the capacity and opportunity to choose for himself the path that may bring him the good that he needs, in order that the application of the Law of Requital to his movement in life might be justified ? The Qur'ān gives the answer in the affirmative :

> Praise the name of Thy Lord, the Most High Who hath created, and balanced all things, Who hath fixed their destinies, and *giveth them guidance.*
>
> (Q. 87:2)

The stages indicated in this verse are those of *Takhliq* (creation), *Taswiyah* (giving form), *Taqdīr* (assignment of role) and *Hidāyat* (guidance). It points out that even as the *Rubūbiyat* of God has provided each object with an appropriate form and appropriate talents and an appropriate role in life, so also it has endowed it with the gift of self-direction or *Hidāyat.*

> Our Lord is He who hath given to everything its mould and the right direction.
>
> (Q. 20:52)

The guidance or *Hidāyat* which the Qur'ān speaks of is of four kinds—instinct, senses, reason, and revelation. The first two are common to all animal life. The third, namely, reason is peculiar to man. But each one of these types has its limitations. Where instinct ceases to function, senses come to aid; and likewise where senses fail, reason offers succour. But reason too has its limitations beyond which it cannot offer guidance to man. It is why, as part of the *Rubūbiyat* of God and of the *Raḥmat* implicit therein, man has been provided, says the Qur'ān, with an unerring guide in the form of divine revelation:

> 'Say: Verily, guidance (Al-Hudā) from God, that is the true guidance.'
>
> (Q. 2:114)

Al-Hudā is the the term by which the divine guidance is designated here. It means the one and the only real way of guidance. It is also styled *Ad-Dīn*, the Way, and also *Al-Islām*, the way of conformity or surrender to the laws of life fixed by God.

Unity of Revelation:

The fundamental basis of the Quranic message is that divine revelation has always remained one and the same. But the vagaries of history are so strange, says Mawlana Azad, that the greater the emphasis that the Qur'ān lays on this truth, the stronger has been the inclination on the part of the world to relegate it to the background. In fact no other truth of the Qur'ān has been kept so deliberately out of sight. Should one study the Qur'ān with an open mind and look into its numerous clear assertions in this respect, and then take a survey of what has actually happened despite such assertions, one will not fail to notice that the faith of the Qur'ān also has in the course of history been given the character of an exclusive concern even as other faiths.

To clarify this issue, Mawlana Azad has found it necessary to explain at some length the Quranic view of revelation or the function of Prophethood and show in what direction the Qur'ān aims to lead the human mind.

The Quranic contention, points out Mawlana Azad, is that mankind were at first but one people and lived but one common natural life. It was only at subsequent stages when they multiplied, and economic pressure gave rise among them to conflict of interests that they came to be divided into groups, each hating the other, so much so, that the situation demanded the delivery of a message of truth such as might re-unite them once again. It was thus that the door of prophethood or revelation was opened, and a series of prophets followed in succession to bring home to mankind the value of unity. The Qur'ān calls these benefactors of mankind as 'Rusl' (Singular, Rasūl') or 'Message bearers' since they brought to mankind the divine message of Truth.

The message of these prophets was one and the same and was not meant for any particular clime or country or people. The Qur'ān states that there is no corner of the world occupied by man where this universal message was not delivered.

> And every people hath its guide.
>
> (Q. 13:8)

The Qur'ān adds that numerous were the messengers who thus delivered the message in the past, though only a few of them were mentioned by name.

> 'And yet how many prophets sent We among those of old.'
>
> (Q. 43:5)

'We never chastised until We had first sent an apostle.'

(Q. 17:16)

'And We have already sent apostles before thee: Of some We have told thee, and of others We have told thee nothing.'

(Q. 40:78)

The way of God is the same in every age. It cannot differ from itself in any circumstance. It has therefore addressed itself to humanity in one and the same fashion. The message was simply this that one should believe in one God and act righteously in consonance with that belief. That was the religion offered to mankind in all ages and in all climes:

'And to every people have We sent an apostle saying: Worship God and turn away from "Ṭāghūt" (that which operates for disturbance in life.)'

(Q. 16:38)

The Qur'ān says that there has been no founder of a religion who has not enjoined the observance of this principle in life and has not discouraged differences therein. The aim has been to bring together those who stood divided. And this was to be achieved through the worship of one common God and a way of life which should enable them to live together in mutual love and affection.

'And truly this your religion is the one religion, and I am your Lord.'

(Q. 23:54)

'To you (Prophet Muhammad) have We prescribed the faith which We commended unto Noah and which We have revealed to thee and which We commended unto Abraham and Moses and Jesus, saying: "Observe this faith and be not divided into sects therein".'

(Q. 42:13)

The Qur'ān asserts that there is no revealed scripture which does not lay stress on the need to follow the way of God that it speaks of:

'Say: Bring forth your proofs. This is the lesson which those who are with me bear in mind, and this the lesson preached by those who came before me: but most people know not the truth, and turn aside. No apostle have We sent before thee to whom We did not reveal that "verily, there is no God beside Me".'

(Q. 21:23-24)

The Qur'ān further asserts that the teaching of one prophet endorses the teaching of another, since the teaching was the same:

'In truth hath He sent down to thee the Book, which confirmeth those which precede it: For, He had sent down the Law and the Evangel aforetime, as man's guidance.'

(Q. 3:2)

AD-DIN AND ASH-SHAR'A

The question arises: If Revelation has laid down but one and the same principle of life, how then come in the differences which exist between one religion and another, and why was not one and the same code of law, conduct and ceremonial prescribed by one and all?

The Qur'ān says that differences in respect of religion are of two kinds. One is that which is the result of a deliberate deviation from the common basic message effected by its followers. This the Qur'ān does not countenance. The other is a difference in the manner of implementing the message. For instance, one religion prescribes a particular form of worship; another a different form. A difference of this nature is not a difference in *Dīn*, but a difference in the way it is given effect to. It is why a difference is to be made between *Dīn* and *Shar'a* or the way of implementing the *Dīn*. The *Dīn* admits of no variation. It is to be the same at all times and for all people. But social aptitudes and conditions of life vary from time to time and country to country, and necessitate variations in the manner and method of implementing the Dīn; and these are permissible so long as they do not contravene the basic belief in the Unity of God and righteous living.

> 'To every people have We appointed observances which they observe. Therefore, let them not dispute this matter with thee, but bid them to their Lord (the basic provision), for thou art on the right way.'
>
> (Q. 22:66)

> 'And for every one has a side to turn to (for prayer). Better therefore vie one with another in good works. God will gather you all together, for God has power over all things.'
>
> (Q. 2:143)

In Sūrat-ul-Mā'ida (Chapter 5), the issue is clarified further. After referring successively to the socio-religious dispensations recommended by Moses, Jesus and the Prophet of Islam, the Chapter proceeds to state:

> 'To each among you have We prescribed a Law and an open way. If God had so willed, He would have made you all of but one pattern; but He would test you by what He hath given to each. Be emulous then in good deeds.'
>
> (Q. 5:52-53)

The above verses bring out clearly the distinction between *Dīn* and *Minhāj* or *Shar'a*. *Dīn* is Devotion to God by good living, and *Shar'a* is the programme followed. The test or criterion by which the programme is to be judged is the nature or quality of the goodness it results in. The Qur'ān presents the essential elements which enter into the composition of religion in the following words:

> 'There is no righteousness in turning your faces towards the East or the West, but he is righteous who believeth in God, and the last day, and the angels, and the Scriptures, and the Prophets; who for the love of God disburseth his wealth to his kindred, and to the orphans, and the needy, and the wayfarer, and those who ask, and for ransoming, who observeth prayer, and payeth the poor-tax, and who is of those who are faithful to their engagements when they have engaged in them, and is patient under ills and hardships, and in time of trouble; these are they who are just, and these are they who fear the Lord.'
>
> (Q. 2:171)

This verse has stood in the Qur'ān for over 1300 years. If the world has still to understand what really constitutes religion, remarks Mawlana Azad, it is certainly not the fault of the Qur'ān.

Unity of Din disregarded

When the Qur'ān was delivered, the followers of the prevailing religions took the outward forms of religion for *Dīn* itself, and all enthusiasm for it was concentrated on ritual. Every group denied salvation to every other merely on the basis of ritual. But ritual was not *Dīn*, said the Qur'ān, nor the criterion of truth. It was merely an outward aspect of it. The spirit was something superior to it, and that alone was *Dīn* or religion. The real *Dīn* was devotion to God and righteous living, and was no exclusive heritage of any single group. On the other hand, it was the common heritage of all mankind. Actions and customs are but secondary to it. They have changed and are liable to change from time to time under varying circumstances. 'To each among you have we prescribed a Law (Shar'a) and an open way (Minhāj)' says the Qur'ān. The term used here is not *Dīn* which should be the same for every one. That admits of no variation. *Shar'a* or *Minhāj* could not therefore have been, from its very nature, uniformly the same for one and all.

It is this which the Qur'ān aims to emphasise whenever it states : 'Had God so willed, He would have made you all of but one pattern.' The statement takes cognizance of the differences in disposition of the different sections of mankind living in different countries resulting in differences in manners, customs and ways of living. But differences of this character are incidental to the nature of man and should not form the criteria of truth and untruth, and result in mutual dislikes and hostilities. Only the basis of religion should not be disturbed, viz., belief in the Unity of God and righteous living.

It is why the Qur'ān lays great stress on the need for tolerance. Indeed, it puts in a word for even those who have violently opposed its very message of the Unity of God.

> 'Revile not those whom they call on beside God, lest they, in their ignorance, despitefully revile Him. We have so fashioned the nature of man that they like the deeds they do. After all, they shall return to their Lord, and He will declare to them what their actions have been.'
> (Q. 6 : 108)

Addressing the Prophet on one occasion, it says :

> 'And if thy Lord had pleased, verily all who are in the earth would have believed together. What ! wilt thou compel men to become believers ?'
> (Q. 10 : 99)

Revival of Message

The question then arises : If the basis of all religions is the same, or if all rest on Truth, what then was the need for the Qur'ān ? It says in reply : Although all religions are based on truth, their followers have turned away from it, and so the need arises to bring them back to it. That is the task of the Qur'ān.

This falling off from *Dīn*, from Truth, states Mawlana Azad, is in the sphere of doctrinal beliefs, as well as, in that of action. Of the several forms which this has taken, the most serious is the falling off from the basis of religion which the Qur'ān styles as *Tashaiyu'* and *Tahadhdhuḅ* or group formation.

> 'As to those who split up the *Dīn* and become sects, have thou nothing to do with them ; their affair

is with God. Hereafter shall He tell them what they have done.'

(Q. 6 : 160)

'But men have rent their great concern (the *Dīn* or the one religion that was meant for all mankind), one among another into sects, every party rejoicing in that which is their own.'

(Q. 23 : 56)

Tashaiyu'

The import of the terms *Tashaiyu'* and *Tahadhdhub* needs to be understood in their proper perspective. The purpose of the *Dīn* divinely specified was to set mankind on the path of devotion to God and of righteous living. This was disregarded. Mankind divided themselves into races and communities each observing customs and manners differing from those of every other. Stress was laid less on faith as the basis of action, than on one's group interest. That came to be the test of truth in religion. Exclusivism thus came into vogue everywhere denying salvation to all except those who belonged to one's own group. In fact, hatred of another's religion replaced devotion to God and righteous living.

Quranic Attitude

The Qur'ān had to dispel these notions. It made faith and deed the sole means of salvation, and not affiliation to any particular group. It asserted that the religion revealed by God was but one for all mankind and that every deviation from it was a negation of religion. It emphasised that real religion was direct worship of but one God, without any mediating agency, and that this was the main teaching of all prophets, and that every belief and practice which conflicted with it amounted to a denial of God.

> And they say, 'None but Jews or Christians shall enter Paradise'. This is their wish. Say: Give your proofs, if ye speak the truth. But they who set their face with resignation Godward, and do what is right,—their reward is with their Lord; no fear shall come on them, neither shall they be grieved.
>
> (Q. 2 : 105-106)

> Verily, they who believe (Muslims) and they who follow the Jewish religion, and the Christians, and the Sabians—whosoever believeth in God and the last day, and doeth that which is right—shall have their reward with their Lord: fear shall not come upon them, neither shall they be grieved.
>
> (Q. 2 : 59)

Religion, according to the Qur'ān, was thus not a name for any groupism. Whatever the race or community or country one belonged to, if only he believed in God and did deeds in consonance with that belief, in other words, lived righteously, he was a follower of the *Dīn* of God, and salvation was his recompense. But the Jews and Christians devised a code of thought and conduct exclusive to themselves. The former drew a circle round them and gave to their exclusivism the name of Judaism. The Christians in their turn drew a like circle round them and called it Christianity. Each held that he who was within their circle was fitted for salvation, and he who was outside of it was doomed. The concept of faith in the God of all humanity and in righteous living was thus side-tracked. One might be an ardent devotee of God, and practise righteous living, but if he happened to be outside of the circle of Judaism or Christianity, no Jew or Christian would regard him as the 'rightly guided'. On the other hand, one might indeed be a wicked person sa lvation was his, if only he was a regular member of their order. The Qur'ān disapproves of this attitude. It proclaims that whatever one's race or community or affiliation, he who offers sincere devotion to God and practises righteous-ness in accordance with that belief, he has attained salvation and no fear shall come upon him. Such is the noble view of universal humanity which the Qur'ān advances. It, however, observes with regret:

> Moreover, the Jews say, 'the Christians lean on nought'. 'On nought lean the Jews', say the Christians : Yet both are readers of the Book. (Old Testament). So with like words say they who have no knowledge. But on the day of resurrection, God shall judge between them as to that in which they differ.
>
> (Q. 2 : 107)

The Jews went so far as even to think that hell-fire would never touch them. The Qur'ān, however, announces that he who does good, good is his reward; and he who does evil, evil is his reward, and that this law of life does not alter for the sake of any particular race or person.

> 'And they say : Fire will not touch us but for a few days. Say : Have you received a promise from Allāh ? Then Allāh will not fail to perform His promise. Or do you speak against Allāh what you know not ? Yes, whoever earns evil

and his sins beset him every side, those are the companions of the Fire; therein they abide'

(Q. 2:74-75)

'It will not be in accordance with your vain desires nor the vain desires of the People of the Book. Whoever does evil, will be requited for it and will not find for himself besides Allāh a friend or a helper.'

(Q. 4:121)

It was one of the results flowing from this group sense that the Jews thought that the law revealed to them enjoining honesty in business transactions was not binding on them in their dealings with the non-Jews. They developed the idea that it was lawful to appropriate as they wished the property of those who did not belong to their group. For instance, the injunction of prohibition of usury was observed by them only in respect of transactions among themselves, and not in their dealings with others. Such was the attitude which the Jews deliberately displayed towards the Arabs of the Prophet's time. They thought that the Arabs were an illiterate people and mere idolators, and that it was right to appropriate to themselves their property by every means at their disposal.

'They took usury, though they were forbidden;
And they devoured men's substance wrongfully.'

(Q. 4:159)

'This—because they say, "we are not bound to keep faith with the ignorant folk." And they utter a lie against God, and know they do so. (For) Whoso is true to his engagement, and feareth God,—Verily God loveth those that fear Him.'

(Q. 3:69-71)

Such an attitude was clearly repugnant to the *Dīn* of God, the revealed law of life which enjoined goodness towards every human being and honest dealing with him, whatever the group to which he belonged.

Among the obsessions which groupism gave rise to, we may refer in particular to the ceremonial called Baptism. Originally this was a Jewish ceremonial which was gone through when one had to admit one's sins and seek forgiveness of God. But the Christian Church converted this into an instrument of salvation. The Qur'ān treats this as a travesty of truth, and points out that salvation cannot be gained by performing a mere ritual and that, on the other hand, salvation comes through righteous living. One must be baptised not by mere water, but by the touch of God, or as the Qur'ān expresses by putting on the 'colour of God' over his thought and action.

> Such is the way, the colour of God, and Who can give that colour better than God Himself.
>
> (Q. 2 : 132)

Thus it w[illegible] although the religion of the two people, the Jews and Christians, was the same, and the Old Testament was the common heritage of both, their division into two groups led to mutual conflict and hatred. One condemned the other and denied salvation to its members.

When the world was so divided into groups, each calling the religion of the other as false, notwithstanding the fact that all were the same at their base, who was to decide who represented the truth? The Qur'ān said that Truth in reality was with every one of them, but that in practice they had neglected it. Each had been given but one and the same *Dīn*, or one and the same universal principle of guidance, but one and all had chosen to disturb its basic character. Instead of adhering to the *Dīn* or the straight path, every group followed a line of its own and appropriated to itself an exclusive right to salvation. The Qur'ān proclaimed that Hidāyat or the Path of divine guidance was open to every one, and was not reserved exclusively for any particular race or people.

> 'Others of the people of the Book say: And believe in those only who follow your Religion. (But you) say: True guidance is guidance from God that to others may be imparted the like of what hath been imparted to you. Will they wrangle then with you in the presence of their Lord.'
>
> (Q. 3 : 66)

CHAPTER VI

UNITY OF MAN

'Will they wrangle with you then in the presence of their Lord?' is the admonition which the Qur'ān deals out to all those who had divided themselves into exclusive religious groups in the name of God. Belief in God, if entertained in sincerity, must, in the field of action, express itself in the Unity of man. That was the cry of the Qur'ān, its call to the Jews, the Christians and the Arab polytheists of the Prophet's time. Its essential mission was to unite them in a common bond once again and pave the way to a wider unity of mankind. Such is the reading of the Quranic mission by Mawlana Azad.

The first item in the programme of unity which the Qur'ān envisaged was to proclaim to one and all that mankind were at first but one community believing in but one God of all mankind, and must therefore pursue a *Dīn* or path of life in accordance with that belief. In the preceding chapter, it has been shown how strenuously the Qur'ān endeavoured to emphasize that this path of life could be but one and the same for one and all. In pursuance of this principle, the Qur'ān addressed itself to the Jews, Christians and Arabs of the day. The one thing common to them all was the respect which they all paid to the memory of Abraham as their common ancestor. A straightforward proposition was therefore advanced by the Qur'ān for their consideration. If the exclusiveness of each of their groups was identical with Truth, it asked, to what group did this common ancestor of theirs belong? In his time, there prevailed neither

Judaism, nor Christianity. What then was the way or the *Dīn* which he followed?

> O people of the Book! why do you dispute about Abraham, when the Torah and the Gospel were not revealed till after him? Do you not understand?
>
> (Q. 3 : 58)

> Or were you witnesses when death visited Jacob when he said to his sons: What will you serve after me? They said: We shall serve thy God And the God of thy fathers, Abraham and Ishmael And Issac, One God only, and to Him do we submit.
>
> (Q. 2 : 127)

> The Jews say: Be a Jew.
> The Christians say: Be a Christian: You will be on the right course.
> Say: Nay, (We follow) the Dīn of Abraham, the upright one, and he was not one of those who identified God with anything else.
>
> (Q. 2 : 129)

The attempt here is to point out that the Jews, the Christians and the rest of the people in Western Asia followed in the time of their ancestor, Abraham, a religion which was neither Judaism nor Christianity nor any other groupism, as the two faiths arose after him in the name of Moses and Jesus who were born several centuries after him, and to show that the path of salvation which Abraham followed was meant not for any exclusive group but for all mankind, *viz.* the path of devotion to but one God and of righteous living. The message which Abraham and every other prophet delivered, states the Qur'ān, was that mankind were in reality one people or one community and that there was but one God for all of them and that on that account they should worship Him together and live as members of but one family. It quotes the utterances of the prophets gone before to show that every one of them had affirmed the unity of Divine Revelation and enjoined that mankind should live together as brothers unto each other, and not live divided. But to the regret of the Qur'ān, 'men rent their great concern one among others into sects, every party rejoicing in that which was their own'.

(Q. 23 : 55)

THE QURANIC CALL

There is nothing in the Qur'ān, says Mawlana Azad, on which so great a stress is laid as on this view of life. It is repeatedly made clear that it does not favour any exclusive group religion. On the other hand, it asserts that it has come to put an end to every form of groupism and bring all mankind to one path of life, the path of truth which, by its very nature, has had to remain the same throughout the course of time, the path to which all prophets have invited.

> 'To you (Prophet Muhammad) hath He presented the faith which we commended unto Noah, and which we have revealed to thee, and which we commended unto Abraham and Moses and Jesus, saying, 'Observe this faith, and be not divided into sects therein'.
>
> (Q. 42-11)

> 'Verily we have revealed to thee as we revealed to Noah and the prophets after him, and as we

revealed to Abraham, and Ishmael, and Isaac, and Jacob, and the tribes and Jesus, and Job and Jonah, Aaron, and Solomon ; and to David gave we Pslams.

Of some apostles we have told thee before: of other apostles we have not told thee—Apostles charged to announce and to warn, that men, after those apostles, might have no plea against God.'

(Q. 4 : 161-163)

'O Ye apostles ! Truly this your religion is the one Religion, and I am your Lord.'

(Q. 23 : 54)

In the *Surat -ul-An'ām* (Chapter 6) referring to the previous prophets, the Qur'ān addresses the prophet Muhammad in the following words:

'These are those whom God has guided.
So follow therefore their guidance.'

(Q. 6 : 90)

As part of the plan to bring the followers of all religions on a single platform, the Qur'ān recognised the founders of all religions as divinely inspired and endorsed their teaching.

'Say: We believe in God, and in what hath been sent down to us, and what hath been sent down to Abraham, and Ishmael and Isaac, and Jacob, and the tribes, and in what was given to Moses, and Jesus, and the Prophets from their Lord. We make no difference between them. And to Him are we resigned.'

(Q. 3 : 78)

The expression 'we make no difference between them' in the above verse recurs in various places in the Qur'ān just to mark its disapproval of the tendency of regarding one prophet as superior to another, or of accepting one prophet and rejecting another as the bearer of truth. The Qur'ān calls upon everyone who cares to follow the way laid down by God to accept without discrimination all the prophets and all the scriptures revealed to them and the basic truth which they all contain, and to accept it wherever found and in whatever language expressed.

> 'The apostle believeth in that which hath been sent down from his Lord, as do the faithful also. They all believe in God and His angels, and His Books, and His apostles: We make no distinction between any of His apostles. And they say 'We have heard and obeyed. Thy mercy, Lord! for unto Thee must we return'.
>
> (Q. 2 : 285)

The divine truth, says the Qur'ān, is an universal gift from God. It is not exclusive to any race or any people or religious group and is not exclusively delivered in any particular language. Men may create for themselves geographical and racial boundaries. But they cannot so divide the divine truth. That truth bears no national stamp, and recognises no racial or geographical loyalties or group affiliations. Like the Sun created of God, it shines in every corner of the globe, and shines equally well on every one. It is noticeable everywhere and has found expression in every age. The Truth of God wherever found and in whatever form is man's treasure and man is heir to it.

The Qur'ān has repeatedly pronounced that discrimination between prophets amounts to a denial of the *Dīn* of God itself which recognises them all without distinction. There are therefore only but two ways open for man. One is the way of recognition of them all: the other is that of rejection. There is no third. The rejection of even one prophet means the rejection of every other as well.

> 'Of a truth they who believe not in God and His apostles, and seek to separate God from His apostles, and say 'some we believe and some we believe not', and desire to take a middle course: These! they are veritable disbelievers! and for the disbelievers have we prepared a shameful punishment. And they who believe in God and His Apostles, and make no difference between them—these! we will bestow on them their reward at last.
> God is Gracious, Merciful!'
>
> (Q. 4 : 149)

In the second chapter of it, the Qur'ān points to the way of true believers.

> 'And who believe in what hath been sent down to thee, and in what hath been sent down before thee, and full faith have they in the life to come:
> These are those who follow the guidance of their Lord. It is they who prosper.'
>
> (Q. 2 : 3-4)

The Qur'ān expresses its surprise to find that even those who hold the view that the Universe is the creation of but One Supreme Being, and that it is He who sustains it, should deny that the spiritual way of life prescribed by Him is but one or has been delivered to man in but one way?

> 'Say: O people of the Book! Do ye not disavow us simply because we believe in God, and in what He hath sent down to us, and in what He sent down aforetime, while most of you are transgressers.'
>
> (Q. 5 : 64)

> 'And surely God is my Lord and your Lord; So serve Him. This is the right path.'
>
> (Q. 19 : 37)

> 'Say: Will ye dispute with us about God when He is our Lord and your Lord? We have the result of our deeds and ye have the result of your deeds, and we are sincerely His.'
>
> (Q. 2 : 133)

It may be noted here that wherever forms of address as employed in the above verses occur, such as: 'God is our and your God'—'Our and your God is but one God'—'Do you dispute with us about God, when your and our God is but one and the same God, and for you (the result of) your deeds and for us (the result of) our own', the aim of the Qur'ān is to emphasize that for one and all there is but one God and that every action has a corresponding result. The Qur'ān therefore asks: Why then all this tension and quarrel in the name of God and religion? Repeatedly does the Qur'ān affirm that its teaching is nothing but this that it calls upon man to believe in God and practice righteous living in conformity with that belief and not to condemn anybody's religion or reject its founder. It says that it confirms the basic message common to all religions and endorses it as its own message. When such is the Quranic attitude, why, asks the Qur'ān, do the followers of other religions declare wa st the Qur'ān ?

The Qur'ān, observes] a Azad, has never asked the followers of other religions to accept it as a new faith altogether. On the other hand, it asks them to return to their own religions by first clearing them of the accretions which have gathered around them, and revive their original faith and adhere to it. Should they do so, the purpose of the Qur'ān is served; for, if once one returns to his own religion in stine purity, he will find that there is nothing tl ut what the Qur'ān itself has come forward to re-present. It says that its message is no new message and that it is the same as the prophets of yore had delivered.

> 'Say: O People of the Book! ye have no ground to stand on, until ye observe the Law and the Evangel, and that which hath been sent down to you from your Lord.
>
> The Book which hath been sent down to thee from thy Lord will certainly increase the rebellion and unbelief of many of ther he not thou troubled for the unbelievers
>
> Verily, they who believe, and the Jews and the Sabeans, and the Christians—whoever of them believeth in God and in the last day, and doth what is right, on them shall come no fear, neither shall they be put to grief.'
>
> (Q. 5 : 72-73)

This is the reason why the Qur'ān has openly praised such of the followers of other faiths as upheld at the time of the advent of the Qur'ān the spirit of their own faiths and lived up to their basic teachings. It only observes that their number was but small, the majority having strayed away from their original faith.

> 'They are not all alike. Of the people of the Scripture there is a staunch community who recite the revelations of Allāh in the night season, falling prostrate (before Him).
> They believe in Allāh and the Last Day, and enjoin right conduct and forbid indecency, and vie one with another in good works. These are of the righteous.
> And whatever good they do, they will not be denied the meed thereof. Allāh is aware of those who ward off (evil).'
>
> (Q. 3 : 109-111)

> 'Some there are among them who act aright. But many of them—how evil are their doings.'
>
> (Q. 5 : 70)

Whenever the Qur'ān stresses that it has come only to confirm the previous revealed scriptures and not to deny them, and calls upon their followers to believe in the Qur'ān also, it does so only to emphasize that the Qur'ān does not present anything antagonistic to their faiths, nor does it aim to turn them away from their own faiths but that it in fact even aids them to remain staunch to them. It therefore asks in astonishment: Why then do they declare war against the Qur'ān or quarrel with it?

For the same reason the Qur'ān uses the term 'Ma'rūf' for goodness and 'Munkar' for evil. 'Enjoin the 'Ma'rūf' and forbid the 'munkar' (31:17) is the injunction of the Qur'ān. The word 'Ma'rūf' is derived from 'arafa' meaning to know what is well-known. 'Munkar' means that which cannot be accepted on all hands. The Qur'ān has used those terms particularly because whatever the differences among mankind, there are certain things which are recognised on all hands to be good, and likewise there are certain things which are denied that appellation or are not good. For instance, all agree that to speak truth is right and to speak untruth is wrong. All agree that honesty is a virtue and dishonesty is a vice. All agree that service to parents, kindliness towards neighbours, care of the poor, and aiding of the oppressed are things good in themselves, and none holds a different view about them. All the religions of the world, all moral codes, all philosophies, all communities, whatever views they may severally advance in other matters, they all hold identical views in respect of these qualities. So asks the Qur'ān : Why then should there be any opposition to it when the Qur'ān enjoins the 'ma'rūf' and forbids the 'munkar?'

The way of God

The Qur'ān says that the line of conduct prescribed here is a law of life as every other law of nature, and one has to conform to it if he cares to profit by it. That is the way of God, the right religion, the law that does not alter for any one, the religion which all the prophets followed and preached. It is this very religion which the Qur'ān styles as Islam, or the path of surrender or conformity to the Laws of life fixed by God :

> 'Turn steadfastly to the path of devotion, to the ways of Allāh, for which He hath fitted man. There is no altering of the ways of Allāh. That is the right religion; but most people know it

not. And ye be turned to Him, and fear Him and observe prayer, and be not of those who unite gods with God: or of those who have split up their religion and have become sects, where every party rejoices in what is their own.'

(Q. 30: 29-30)

It is this Islam so continuously delivered throughout the ages which is the true religion or way of life as fixed by God,—the 'Straight Path' which the Qur'ān points to in the *Sūrat-ul-Fātiḥa*, by following which individuals, as well as, communities achieve goodness or success in life or, to use the Quranic phraseology 'Win the approbation of God', and by neglecting which, perish or receive in rec disapprobation. If the different groups into which mankind has divided itself should resolve to return to the path of devotion to God and of righteous living—the religion once vouch-safed to one and all—by discarding all the sectarian touches given to it in the course of history, the purpose of the Qur'ān is fulfilled. It has no other aim.

'The true religion with God is Islam: and they to whom the Scriptures had been given, differed not till after 'the knowledge' had come to them, and through mutual jealousy. But as for him who shall not believe in the signs of God—God will be prompt to reckon with him.

If they shall dispute with thee, then say: I have surrendered myself to God, as have they who follow me.

Say to those who have received the Book, and to the common folk: "Do ye surrender yourselves unto God?" If they surrender, they are those who are guided aright: but if they turn away—

> thy duty is only preaching; and G(is
> on his servants'
>
> (Q. 3: 17-19)

The Qur'ān points out that Religion lies in strictly following the moral law implicit in life. In fact, the entire creation rests on that basis. The slightest urge on the part of creation to stray away from the prescribed path will result in the collapse of the entire machinery of life.

> 'Other ways than the way of God desire they? To Him doth everything that is in the heavens and in the earth submit in willing or forced obedience! and to Him do they return.'
>
> (Q. 3: 77)

When the Qur'ān states that *Al-Islām* or the path of acquiescence in the way of God, or of obedience or conformance to it, is the only religion favoured of God and was the religion which every Prophet delivered, every other way or religion is bound to be groupism of some sort and not the universal way of God.

> 'And whose seeketh as religion other than the path of surrender (to God), it will not be accepted from him, and he will be a loser in consequence.'
>
> (Q. 3: 79)

It was why, the Qur'ān repeatedly called upon all those who had responded to its message not to cut their religion into sects again or return to the darkness from which the Qur'ān had rescued them. It pointed out that it had brought those who ghting each other to the path of devotion to G welded them into a brotherhood. It had lined up in a single file those who had once hated each other—the Jews, the Christians, the Magians and the Sabeans—and made them recognise together the founders of the faiths which they severally professed.

> 'And hold fast, all of you together, by the cable of God, and break not loose from it, and remember God's goodness towards you, how when ye were enemies, He united your hearts and by His grace ye became brethren; and when ye were on the brink of an abyss of fire, He drew you back from it. Thus God clearly showeth you His signs, that ye may be guided.'
>
> (Q. 3: 98-99)

> 'And be ye not like those who have formed divisions, and fallen to variance after the clear proofs had come to them. These! A terrible chastisement doth await them.'
>
> (Q. 3: 101)

> 'And (He commandeth you, saying): 'This is My straight path, so, follow it'. Follow not other ways, lest ye be parted from His way. This hath He enjoined that ye may ward off (evil).'
>
> (Q. 6: 154)

The Basis of Opposition to the Qur'an :

To clarify the issue still further, Mawlana Azad proceeds to describe the nature of the opposition offered in the time of the Prophet to this message of the Qur'ān by the followers of the religions which then prevailed in Arabia. Some of them possessed revealed scriptures. Did the Qur'ān deny any scriptures? Did it claim that it alone was the repository of truth, and that therefore the followers of other faiths should give up the

Prophets in whom they had believed till then? Did it present anything absolutely novel, so that they should hesitate to accept it? None of these questions could validly be levelled against it, observes Mawlana Azad. The Qur'ān offered its recognition, says he, not only to the Prophets in whom the followers of other faith specifically believed, but to all the prophets that ever arose to deliver the message of God. It did not discriminate between them. It never called upon any one to give up one's religion. On the other hand, it pursuaded every one to return to one's original belief in the Unity of God and righteous living, since this was the basis of all religions. It neither presented a new principle of life, nor a new line of action unknown before. It only emphasised that all religions enjoined but one way of life, the way of devotion to God and of righteous living. It therefore called upon them to revive their own religions in the light of this common basic purpose and live in fraternal relations with each other. To do so was indeed to accept the message of the Qur'ān.

Why then was there any opposition at all to the Qur'ān? The Qur'āish of Mecca did not like it, because it expressed itself against idolatry. But what reason had the Jews to turn away from it when the Jews were not idolators? Why did the Christians go into opposition also when they never claimed to support idolatry. The followers of each faith desired that the Qur'ān should declare the faith of their rivals as false. And since the Qur'ān would not do it, no one was pleased with it. Of course, the Jews rejoiced to see that the Qur'ān openly endorsed recognition to their Prophet Moses. But since the Qur'ān at the same time accorded recognition to Christ, the Jews would necessarily oppose it. The Christians in their turn were happy to know from the Qur'ān that it upheld the purity of the life of Mary, the mother of Jesus. But they were angry with it when it rested salvation on faith and righteous action and not on baptism or the atonement of Christ on the Cross. That was too much for the Christians to bear. Similarly, the Meccans were happy to know that the Qur'ān held in high estimation the prophets Abraham and Ishmael who belonged to their race. But they felt uncomfortable whenever the Qur'ān at the same time eulogized the Jewish Prophets who did not belong to them.

In short, there were three distinct principles of the Qur'ān which displeased the followers of the prevailing faiths of the time in Arabia.

Firstly, the Qur'ān was opposed to groupism. It proclaimed the unity of religion. If this was conceded, it would knock the bottom out of every form of groupism which emphasized that salvation truly lay with one's own group and with no other.

Secondly, the Quranic assertion was that salvation was the result of devotion to God and righteous living, and did not rest on any racial or group affiliation, or on the observance of any particular ceremonial. The acceptance of this principle would have opened the door of salvation to every human being, and this the followers of the faiths of that time would not concede.

And *thirdly*, the Qur'ān asserted that religion lay in direct devotion to God without any mediating agency. But the followers of the other faiths had in one form or other developed the institution of idolatry in the name of devotion to God. They did profess that true devotion was direct, but they would not give up the practice which they had inherited from their forbears and to which they were deeply attached.

To sum up

me of the advent of the Qur'ān, religious had not overstepped the group consciousness of the different peoples of the world. Each religious gro ned that its own religion was the true religion it salvation was only for those who professed it. The criterion of truth was the character of the ceremonial and of the s and manners which the followers of a religion of such as the form of worship or the ceremonial attendant on sacrifices, the type of food permitted or prohibited, and the outward mode of dress or manner of living. Since the outer form of faith and living of one group was different from that of every other, the follower of each group decried, on that account, the religion of every other. The claim of every religious group was not merely that it alone was the bearer of truth, but that the religion of every other group was false. The natural result of such an attitude was hatred of others and mut bloodshed in the name of God.

The Qur'ān came forward to present to the world at large the principle of Unity in religion. It advanced the view that even as the laws of Nature regulated and sustained the machinery of the Uni there was a al law of life to govern , and that this law was one and the same for every one. The greatest error into which mankind fell was to forget and disregard this spiritual law of life and to divide mankind into rival camps. The primary aim of this spiritual law of life or the way of God, the *Dīn*, was to keep mankind united and not to serve as a force for disunity. The greatest tragedy of man was that he turned a ment of unity, viz., religion, into a weapon of dis

The Qur'ān came to distinguish religion proper from

its outward observance. The former it called *Dīn*, and the latter *Shar'a* and *Minhāj*. *Dīn* was but one and the same everywhere and at all times, and was vouchsafed to one and all without discrimination. In respect of the outward observance of the *Dīn*, there was variation and this was inevitable. It varied from time to time and from people to people as warranted by varying situations. Variations of this nature could not alter the character of the *Dīn* or the basis of religion. That was the truth which the Qur'ān aimed to emphasise. Its complaint was that *Dīn* had been neglected and variation in *Shar'a* and *Minhāj* or the outward form of observance idealized and made the basis of differences among mankind.

The Qur'ān announced in very clear terms that its function was but to proclaim that all religions, as first delivered, upheld but one Truth, but that their followers disregarded it. Should they return to this neglected Truth, or to the principle of devotion to God and of righteous living, the mission of the Qur'ān was fulfilled. The act would be regarded as indeed the acceptance of the Qur'ān. The truth common to all of them was what was styled *Ad-Dīn* or *Al-Islām*. It observed that the *Dīn* of God was not meant to divide man from man, but that, on the other hand, it was there to inspire the feeling of fellowship between one and another and let them all live together bound by the common tie of devotion to God.

The evil of groupism is at work everywhere even today. But how to get rid of it? The evil has crept in because the basis of religion has been kept out of sight. It is now for the followers of each groupism to retrace their steps and return to the basic teaching of each religion, the *Dīn* common to all. If that were done, says the Qur'ān, all disputes will be set at rest, and every one will begin to see that the way of all religions is but one and the same viz., the one *Dīn* or way meant for all mankind and to which the Qur'ān gives the name of *Al-Islām*, or the way of peace, as translated literally, or of devotion to God and of righteous living. That is the only way to restore the forsaken sense of humanity to mankind or revive the idea that for all of us there is but one Providence, and that we should all in unity bow our heads at his threshold only and develop a feeling of unity and solidarity such as shall overcome and dispel from our midst all differences coined by ourselves in the course of history. That such was the purpose of the Qur'ān is clear from the call which went forth to members of all faiths during the time of the Prophet.

> 'O People of the Book (Revealed Scriptures) come to a word fair between us and you, that we worship God only and associate nothing with Him, and do not take each other as Lord to the exclusion of God.' (Q. 3:57)

The Qur'ān here offers a federal principle for the unification of the human race. It may not be possible to weld the entire world into a single pattern by prescribing a common *Shar'a* or a code of social laws for one and all, or a common mode of worship. It only asks mankind to forge a nexus for human society so that believing in one God of all humanity, the several nations of the Earth might enter into fraternal or federal relations with one another and enjoy the good things of the Earth righteously as members of a single family, the 'Family of God', as described by the Prophet, or 'a Fold every member of which shall be a shepherd unto every other and be accountable for the welfare of the entire fold'.

Such has been the standing message of the Qur'ān for over thirteen hundred years!

INDEX

INDEX

INDEX

www.ingramcontent.com/pod-product-compliance
Lightning Source LLC
Chambersburg PA
CBHW062141160726
48282CB00027B/898
* 9 7 8 9 3 6 6 0 8 9 4 0 9 *